SHAKESPEARE

SHAKESPEARE

•

Germaine Greer

A BRIEF
INSIGHT

STERLING

New York / London
www.sterlingpublishing.com

STERLING and the distinctive Sterling logo are registered trademarks of
Sterling Publishing Co., Inc.

Library of Congress Cataloging-in-Publication Data

Greer, Germaine, 1939-
  Shakespeare : a very short introduction / Germaine Greer.
      p. cm. -- (Brief insights)
  Includes index.
  ISBN 978-1-4027-7533-8
  1. Shakespeare, William, 1564-1616. I. Title.
  PR2894.G75 2010
  822.3'3--dc22

                              2009039601

10 9 8 7 6 5 4 3 2 1

Published by Sterling Publishing Co., Inc.
387 Park Avenue South, New York, NY 10016

Published by arrangement with Oxford University Press, Inc.

© 1986 by Germaine Greer
Illustrated edition published in 2010 by Sterling Publishing Co., Inc.
Additional text © 2010 Sterling Publishing Co., Inc.

Distributed in Canada by Sterling Publishing
c/o Canadian Manda Group, 165 Dufferin Street
Toronto, Ontario, Canada M6K 3H6

Book design: The DesignWorks Group

Please see picture credits on page 199 for image copyright information.

Printed in China
All rights reserved

Sterling ISBN 978-1-4027-7533-8

For information about custom editions, special sales, premium and corporate purchases, please contact
Sterling Special Sales Department at 800-805-5489 or specialsales@sterlingpublishing.com.

Frontispiece: This painting of Shakespeare is called the Chandos portrait after its one-time owner
James Brydges, third Duke of Chandos. The portrait may have been painted by John Taylor (ca.
1585–1651), a former child actor, and was bought in 1856 by the National Portrait Gallery in London—
its first acquisition.

CONTENTS

•

ONE

Life

●

THE NOTICES OF THE LIFE AND CAREER of England's greatest poet are not only sparse and brief, but unusually cryptic. If ever their meaning was precisely understood it is so no longer. All attempts to break the unselfconscious code have failed. The name Shakespeare, in one form or another, was a common one in sixteenth-century Warwickshire. The poet was probably the grandson of Richard Shakespeare, a husbandman of Snitterfield, a hamlet four miles to the north of Stratford. It is assumed that the "Johannem Shakesper de Snytterfyld . . . agricolam" who was

On March 9, 2009, officials at the Shakespeare Birthplace Trust unveiled what they said was the only portrait of Shakespeare to have been painted from life—the so-called Cobbe Portrait, named after the Anglo-Irish Cobbe family, who acquired it in the early eighteenth century. But the work is almost certainly a version of a portrait of the British essayist Sir Thomas Overbury (1581–1613) painted by Marcus Gheeraerts, the original of which resides in the Bodleian Library. The young, handsome Overbury—unlike Shakespeare, a courtier, as the clothing in this portrait indicates—was poisoned while he was imprisoned in the Tower of London, and his murder was never solved. The Overbury case was a famous scandal with political ramifications, and Overbury's likeness was much in demand.

This photograph shows Shakespeare's birthplace in Henley Street in Stratford-upon-Avon, England, which is owned and managed by the Shakespeare Birthplace Trust. The building and grounds are open to the public.

named administrator of his father's estate in 1561 is the same John Shakespeare who already figures in the records as having been fined for keeping a dung-heap in front of his house in Henley Street in 1552 (the house that is still revered as the Birthplace) and who in a suit of 1556 is described as a glover.

When Richard Arden, Richard Shakespeare's Snitterfield landlord, drew up his will in 1556, his youngest daughter Mary was still single. In 1558, her first child by John Shakespeare was baptized in Holy Trinity Church, Stratford. There her third child was christened, on April 26, 1564, "Gulielmus filius Johannes Shakespeare." From that day nothing is heard of him for more than eighteen years.

John Shakespeare prospered. Although illiterate, he was named one of the chief burgesses, then chamberlain, then alderman in 1565, and

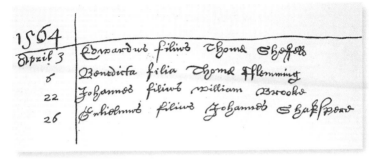

This portion of the baptismal register of the Stratford Parish Church shows the following entry, in Latin, for April 26, 1564: "*Gulielmus filius Johannes Shakspere*" (William, son of John Shakespeare).

finally High Bailiff in 1568. We know from allusions in the plays that Shakespeare must have had at least a grammar-school education, and we assume that as the son of an alderman, and therefore entitled to education free of charge, he must have attended the Stratford grammar school, but the school archives for the period have not survived. From 1578 onward, John Shakespeare began to find himself in financial difficulties. In 1586, after ten years of absence from council meetings, his name was finally struck off the list of aldermen.

On November 27, 1582, the clerk noted in the Episcopal Register of the Diocese of Worcester the application for a special marriage license "inter Willelmum Shaxpere et Annam Whateley de Temple Grafton." The bond posted the next day clearly identifies the groom as William Shagspere and the bride as Anne Hathwey of Stratford. Even in so straightforward a business, Shakespeare has left an unusually puzzling trail which would lead some scholars off on a wild goose chase for "the other woman"; nowadays the discrepancy is usually taken to be merely the result of a scribal error. From the brass marker on Ann Hathaway's grave, which gives her age as sixty-seven when she died in

1623, we know that in 1582 she must have been about twenty-six. The special license was required for a number of reasons: the groom was a minor, the penitential season of Advent when marriages might not be solemnized was only five days away, Ann's father was dead, and she was pregnant. Of all of these circumstances the most unusual is William's age: he was not yet nineteen.

Six months later the Shakespeares' first child, Susanna, was baptized, on May 26, 1583. On February 2, 1585, her brother and sister, the twins Hamnet and Judith, were baptized. Eleven years later the parish register records the burial of the poet's only son.

The years following the baptism of his children and preceding Shakespeare's emergence as a figure in the theatrical world of London are called the "lost" years. Theories abound: Shakespeare might have worked as a schoolmaster, have trained for the law, have gone for a soldier, have traveled in Europe in the train of some great man, have been arrested for stealing deer and fled to London. The next clear mention of him is hardly auspicious. As Robert Greene, decayed scholar-playwright, lay dying of his own excesses, filthy, verminous and destitute, in a borrowed bed, he penned a last pamphlet, *Greenes Groatesworth of Wit bought with a Million of Repentance* (1592). In it he apostrophized his fellow university wits, Marlowe, Nashe, and Peele: "There is an Upstart Crow, beautified with our feathers, that with his *Tiger's heart wrapt in a player's hide*, supposes he is as well able to bombast out a blank verse as the rest of you; and being an absolute *Johannes Fac Totum*, is in his own conceit the only Shakescene in a country."

From Greene's twisted version of a line from *Henry VI Part III*, we know not only that the Henry VI plays must have been performed by this time, but also that they must have had a certain success. Shakespeare is clearly the person referred to, but what is not clear is the nature of the offense of which he is being accused. As an actor reciting lines written by the university men, Shakespeare could not have merited such a venomous attack. If Greene is using the image of the crow as Horace does in his third epistle, which Greene and his fellow graduates must have known well, then he is accusing Shakespeare of passing off the work of others as his own.

Greene died before anyone could find out exactly what he meant. Nashe dissociated himself from such "a scald, trivial, lying pamphlet." Shakespeare evidently took the trouble to speak to Henry Chettle, who had prepared the fair copy of Greene's work for the publisher, and Chettle apologized handsomely to him in the preface to his own *Kind-Heart's Dream* published a few months later. "I am as sorry as if the original fault had been my fault, because myself have seen his demeanor no less civil than he excellent in the quality he professes. Besides, divers of worship have reported his uprightness of dealing, which argues his honesty, and his facetious grace in writing, that approves his art." Clearly Chettle had understood the accusation to be one of plagiarism, but as a refutation his words leave something to be desired. We learn that Shakespeare had refined and agreeable manners and upper-class friends who were prepared to take his part, together with a certain literary talent. There is no good reason for supposing sixteenth-century commercial theater to be any less protean than that of the twentieth century, where plays are not so much written as rewritten in performance. As a successful actor, Shakespeare may well have turned to the university wits for additional material and felt perfectly free to revise what they provided in production. The copying out of plays was a laborious business; usually the actors' parts were written out with their cues, while the stage manager worked from a "platt" listing cue lines and exits and entrances. There can seldom have been an entire copy to spare for a publisher, and besides, the players' companies reckoned their playbooks among their chief assets. Many plays were never published, and many were published anonymously. Few were ascribed to single authors, unless the authors were particularly well known, in which case their names appeared on plays they had nothing to do with.

This portrait of the playwright John Fletcher (1579–1625)—Shakespeare's collaborator on *The Two Noble Kinsmen*, among other works—is a late-seventeenth-century copy of a presumably earlier original dated around 1620. The artist is unknown.

Thomas Heywood claimed to have worked on at least 220 plays, many of which, he said, "by shifting and change of the companies have been negligently lost." Henry Chettle wrote thirteen plays, of which one survives, and collaborated on thirty-six others, of which four have survived. If Shakespeare, as is thought, collaborated with Heywood, Dekker, Munday, and Chettle on *The Book of Sir Thomas More* at some time in the 1590s it is not farfetched to assume that all four, and perhaps others whose names have perished, were at some time called upon to provide material for him. The only serious contender for the title of Shakespeare's collaborator is John Fletcher, whose hand is detected on internal stylistic grounds in *Henry VIII*, who is named as coauthor of *The Two Noble Kinsmen* on the title page of the 1634 quarto, and again as coauthor with Shakespeare of a lost play *Cardenio* in the Stationers' Register (1653). The evidence is far from conclusive, but if conclusive proof of collaboration should be found, it would not invalidate Shakespeare's claim to be the greatest playwright in the English language, however much consternation it might cause to bardolators who have always sought to elevate him to the lonely eminence of prodigious originality. His strength is very much the strength of his time and his milieu; although he transformed everything he found and the greatness of that transformation cannot be exaggerated, the culture of his contemporaries afforded him some remarkable resources. Centuries of the most diligent sifting have not produced a play or any part of a play in his own hand, unless we count the additions to *The Book of Sir Thomas More*.

An essential aspect of the mind and art of Shakespeare, then, is his lack of self-consciousness. Nothing but a complete lack of interest in self-promotion, from which the careful publication of *Venus and Adonis* and *The Rape of Lucrece* are the only aberrations, can explain

Henry Wriothesley (pronounced "Rise-ley"), third Earl of Southampton (1573–1624), was an important patron of Shakespeare. This portrait, attributed to John de Critz the Elder, portrays the earl during his 1603 imprisonment in the Tower of London, where he was incarcerated for his support of the Essex rebellion—an attempt by Robert Devereux, second Earl of Essex (see page 165), to help James VI of Scotland seize the throne from Queen Elizabeth I.

Shakespeare's invisibility. The lives of lesser men and women, insignificant members of his own family, the actors he worked with, the politicians and courtiers he knew or might have known, have all been scrutinized minutely, their every action tracked to find the spoor of the Bard, but they have yielded all but that.

The years 1591–94 were marked by outbreaks of plague which gathered to a head in the summer of 1592. "For the avoiding of concourse of people whereby the infection of pestilence might have increased" in London, the Bartholomew Fair which fell on August 24 was canceled and the theaters closed down. Shakespeare turned his hand to more literary endeavors; in April 1593, *Venus and Adonis* was entered in the Stationers' Register, and in June, Richard Field, a Stratford man, published it. Its dutiful dedication to the young Earl of Southampton was signed with the poet's full name. A year later, *The Rape of Lucrece* appeared, again with a signed dedicatory epistle to Southampton, couched in terms which might be thought to indicate a growing intimacy. "What I have done is yours, what I have to do is yours, being part in all I have, devoted, yours."

TO THE RIGHT
HONOVRABLE, HENRY
VVriothefley, Earle of Southhampton,
and Baron of Titchfield.

 H E loue I dedicate to you Lordfhip is without end:wherof this Pamphlet without beginning is but a fuperfluous Moity. The warrant I haue of your Honourable difpofition, not the worth of my vntutord Lines makes it affured of acceptance. VVhat I haue done is yours, what I haue to doe is yours, being part in all I haue, deuoted yours. VVere my worth greater, my duety would fhew greater, meane time, as it is, it is bound to your Lordfhip; To whom I with long life ftill lengthned with all happineffe.

Your Lordfhips in all duety.

William Shakefpeare,

A ι

Shakespeare's narrative poem *The Rape of Lucrece* was published in 1594 with this effusive dedication to the earl of Southampton.

Both poems enjoyed considerable popularity, if the number of subsequent editions is any guide. *Venus and Adonis* was reprinted eight times during Shakespeare's lifetime, and fourteen times altogether before the Interregnum, that is to say, more often even than the *Arcadia* or Marlowe's *Hero and Leander*. *Lucrece* went through eight editions. We may infer from this that Shakespeare was well known as a poet: whether he was equally recognized as a playwright is another question.

We shall never know if Shakespeare was tempted by the prospect of life as Southampton's protégé, or, indeed, if the option was ever open to him. If the sonnets are any guide, he may have been passed over for someone more brilliant and congenial who was not repelled by the seamier side of Southampton's personality. Whatever the case, it seems that there was little or no suspension of his writing for the theaters. Before the Earl of Pembroke's company of players broke up in the summer of 1593, they had been playing plays by Shakespeare. The 1594 quarto of *Titus Andronicus* says that it had been played by Pembroke's Men and by the servants of the Earl of Derby, Lord Strange, also known as the Admiral's Men, whose playlists show Shakespeare titles playing at the Theatre. The title page of *Titus Andronicus* claims that it had been played also by the Earl of Sussex's servants, who had apparently acquired the plays used by Pembroke's Men and staged them from December 1593 to February 1594. There is no mention of Shakespeare's name. Nor did his name appear on the quarto of *Henry VI Part II* when it appeared as *The First part of the Contention betwixt the two famous Houses of York and Lancaster* in 1594, nor on Part III which appeared as *The true Tragedie of Richard Duke of York* the following year. Awareness of the authorship of plays was generally low, as might be expected when constant adaptation and collaboration were the rule, but in 1598, when the second quarto of *Richard III* was issued, it bore

Shakespeare's name in full on the title page. A second quarto of *Love's Labor's Lost*, issued to replace a bad quarto now lost, announced that it had been "newly corrected and augmented by W. Shakespere." A second quarto of *Richard II* also bore Shakespeare's name in full. We may perhaps infer that by 1598, Shakespeare's name was recognized by publishers as a selling point. Even so Shakespeare's name did not appear on *Henry IV Part I* until its third publication in 1599. The second quarto of *Romeo and Juliet*, which appeared two years after the first in 1599, did not bear his name. The quartos of *Henry IV Part II*, *The Merchant of Venice*, *Midsummer Night's Dream*, and *Much Ado About Nothing*, all published in 1600, all bore his name, but *Henry V*, published the same year, did not. Such seeming haphazardness is the rule in this period, when the name of the company who staged the play was a better selling point than the name of the author.

William Dethick, Garter King of Arms at the College of Arms (a branch of the royal household), granted a coat of arms to Shakespeare in 1596. This document shows a draft of the heraldic design, including the motto "*Non sanz droict*" (not without right).

Before he had any reputation as a playwright, Shakespeare evidently achieved some eminence as an actor, for we find him named as leader with Richard Burbage of a new company, the Lord Chamberlain's Men, in the Declared Accounts of the Royal Chamber for March 15, 1595, when they collected a fee for a Christmas entertainment. In 1596, John Shakespeare was granted a coat of arms, presumably at the instance of his successful son. The next year William Shakespeare bought New Place, a fine old house built by Sir Hugh Clopton, the Stratford boy who had become Lord Mayor of London in 1491, and his family settled there. Thereafter, Shakespeare figures frequently in the Stratford records, as a prosperous citizen with valuable stores of scarce commodities and money to invest in land and houses. Not one of the contemporary references to him in the Stratford records makes any mention of his activity as either poet or playwright.

In 1598 we find Shakespeare's name at the head of the cast list for a performance of Ben Jonson's *Every Man in His Humor* by the Lord Chamberlain's Men at the Curtain. The company was looking for a site to build a new theater, the Globe, out of the timbers of the Theatre, which had been torn down. A piece of land in Bankside was leased to them by the son of Sir Thomas Brend, whose post-mortem accounts name Shakespeare as the principal tenant. According to the lease, dated February 21, 1599, Shakespeare held one-fifth of a half, the other half being shared between the Burbage brothers. After Will Kempe left the company to undertake his famous dance to Norwich, Shakespeare's share of the leasehold increased to a seventh. The records show him living in various bachelor lodgings in Bishopsgate, near the Shoreditch playhouses, in 1596, and later that year on the South Bank; in 1599 the tax records show him living in the Liberty of the Clink, near the Globe. Other players had settled their families in London, but Shakespeare preferred to invest in a great house in his home town, taking temporary accommodation close to his work. Rather than indicating a degree of estrangement from Ann Shakespeare, this arrangement implies that the Shakespeares had a mutual interest in running a big country establishment. Apart from the house itself, which needed considerable restoration, and the baking, brewing, distilling, and other manufacturing activities associated with a large Elizabethan household, there were two barns and two gardens, one at least planted with grape vines. Over the years were added another cottage and garden, and 107 acres of arable land, farmed by tenants. Shakespeare's success in these dealings could not have come about without the intelligent cooperation of his wife.

In 1598 Shakespeare's reputation as poet, player, and playwright reached its zenith. In his *Poems in Divers Humors*, Richard Barnfield praised Shakespeare's "honey-flowing vein," and in his *Palladis Tamia* of the same year, Francis Meres included "A Comparative Discourse of our modern poets with the Greek, Latin, and Italian Poets" in which he paid Shakespeare the highest compliment of which a university man might be supposed capable:

> The sweet witty soul of Ovid lives in mellifluous and honey-tongued Shakespeare, witness his *Venus and Adonis*, his *Lucrece*, his sugared sonnets among his private friends, &c. As Plautus and Seneca are accounted the best for comedy and tragedy among the Latins, so Shakespeare among the English is the most excellent in both kinds for the stage; for comedy witness his *Gentlemen of Verona*, his *Errors*, his *Love Labor's Lost*, his *Love Labor's Won*, his *Midsummer's Night Dream*, and his *Merchant of Venice*; for tragedy, his *Richard*

the Second, Richard the Third, Henry the Fourth, King John, Titus Andronicus, and his *Romeo and Juliet.*

If the compliment seems fulsome, it must be remembered that Meres has higher praise and more of it for Shakespeare's fellow Warwickshireman, Michael Drayton. Meres's comments are particularly valuable because they give us a *terminus ad quem* for twelve plays, one of which cannot now be identified, and for at least some of the sonnets which were circulating in manuscript. In 1599 William Jaggard, hungry to exploit the Shakespeare vogue, put together a collection of poems which he called *The Passionate Pilgrim By W. Shakespeare*; of the twenty poems in the book only five are by Shakespeare. Two of those are versions of Sonnets CXXXVIII and CXLIV, and three are versions of the poetical efforts of the young lords in *Love's Labor's Lost.* The existence of two different title pages might suggest that someone, perhaps Shakespeare himself, perhaps Barnfield, Bartholomew Griffin, or another of the plundered authors, suggested that a second title be inserted omitting any reference to Shakespeare. In 1612, when Jaggard had the temerity to try the same trick again, this time including mangled extracts from Thomas Heywood's *Troia Heroica*, Heywood tells us in an epistle to his printers in his *Apology for Actors* that, as his lines were unworthy of Shakespeare, the greater poet was "much offended with M. Jaggard (that altogether unknown to him presumed to make so bold with his name)."

Modern dating tends to show a slackening in Shakespeare's play production over the last years of Elizabeth's reign, when he produced a play a year, *Hamlet* in 1600, *Twelfth Night* in 1601, *Troilus and Cressida* in 1602, and *King Lear* in 1604. Certainly the frenzied publishing activity of 1598–1600 slowed down. Quartos of *The Merry Wives of*

Windsor, Henry V, and the perennial favorite *Richard III* appeared in 1602; *Hamlet* was published twice in 1603 and 1604. Thereafter, apart from sporadic reappearances of new editions of old plays, for example, *Richard III* (1605, 1612), *Love's Labor's Lost* (1607), *Richard II* (1608, 1615), *Romeo and Juliet* (1609), *Hamlet* (1611), only four new plays were presented, *King Lear* (1608), *Troilus and Cressida* and *Pericles* (1609) and *Othello* (1622). Of the thirteen plays Shakespeare wrote for the King's Men, only *King Lear* and *Pericles* were published in his lifetime (1609). On the other hand, Shakespeare's name appears during this period on the title pages of quartos of plays he did not write, such as *The London Prodigal* (1605) and *A Yorkshire Tragedy* (1608), both of which were supposed to have been staged by the King's Men. These anomalies may be partly explained by a struggle on the part of the Lord Chamberlain's/King's Men to keep their playbooks out of circulation,

The actor Richard Burbage (ca. 1567–1619), seen in this ca. 1600 portrait painted by an unknown artist—possibly Burbage himself—was Shakespeare's partner in the Lord Chamberlain's Men (later known as the King's Men). Burbage was well known as the first interpreter of some of Shakespeare's greatest roles.

for the late quartos are mostly either surreptitious editions of corrupt versions of the play texts or authorized texts issued to supersede pirated versions. If this is the case, we must assume that the measures taken by the King's Men to protect their chief asset were eventually successful. Of the thirty-six plays in the 1623 folio, half had never been printed before. We can probably infer from the misattributions and the continuing editions of *Lucrece* and *Venus and Adonis* that Shakespeare's name was as much a selling point as ever.

In 1601 Shakespeare contributed to a collection of poems called *Love's Martyr: or Rosaline's Complaint*: this puzzling volume may have been compiled as a tribute to the long-married Sir John Salisbury and his wife, or in celebration of a wedding, or as a disguised lament for the fall of Essex (and his lieutenant, the Earl of Southampton, Shakespeare's patron). The principal poem by Robert Chester is preceded by "Divers poetical Essays on the former subject; viz. the Turtle and the Phoenix"; two of these were by Jonson, and one each by Marston, Chapman, and Shakespeare.

"The Phoenix and the Turtle" is the most perfect statement of the Platonic ideal in English poetry. A story circulating among law students in the Middle Temple, recorded in his diary for March 13, 1601, by John Manningham, who had it from Edward Curle, describes Shakespeare as a lover of a different kidney:

Upon a time when Burbage played Richard III there was a citizen grew so far in liking with him that, before she went from the play, she appointed him to come that night unto her by the name of Richard the Third. Shakespeare, overhearing their conclusion, went before, was entertained and at his game ere Burbage came. Then message being brought that Richard the Third was at the door, Shakespeare caused return to be made that William the Conqueror was before Richard the Third.

We have no way of knowing whether the story is true or not, but evidently the young men of the Inns of Court, who were enthusiastic playgoers, found it quite plausible. It is probably quite true to the impression that the man Shakespeare made on them and it is certainly in keeping with the bawdy strain which reappears again and again in the plays, much to the discomfiture of scholars of thinner blood. And, of course, it is not in the least incompatible with Platonic idealism.

The dating of the plays which Shakespeare wrote between 1598, when Meres's list appeared, and 1604, when new plays and revivals of old ones begin to be mentioned in the Revels Accounts, is only fitfully illuminated by such coincidences as an admiring note which Gabriel Harvey wrote on the margin of his Chaucer: "The younger sort take much delight in Shakespeare's *Venus and Adonis*: but his Lucrece, and his tragedy of *Hamlet, Prince of Denmark* have it in them to please the wiser sort." That the play pleased more than just the "wiser sort" may be inferred from an envious aside by the poetaster Anthony Scoloker, speaking of "*Friendly Shakespeare's Tragedies*, where the *Comedian* rides, when the *Tragedian* stands on tiptoe; Faith it should please all, like Prince *Hamlet*." The pirating of the play in 1603 bears further testimony to its success; a superior version followed in 1604. One or other version must have provided the script for an amateur performance by the crew of an East Indiaman anchored off Sierra Leone in 1607.

On May 19, 1603, the new king, James I, evidently on condition that his countryman Lawrence Fletcher be taken into the company, granted Shakespeare and his fellow players a formal Patent under the Great Seal of England. This licensed them "freely to use and exercise the art and faculty of playing comedies, tragedies, histories, interludes, morals, pastorals, stage-plays, and such others, like as they have already studied, or hereafter shall use or study." The Lord Chamberlain's Men had become the King's Men. Shakespeare's name appears at the head of the list of players who were provided with red cloth to make new liveries to wear as Grooms of the King's Chamber in the coronation procession. The Revels Accounts for 1604–5 show performances of six plays by Shakespeare, of which three, *Measure for Measure,* "The Play of Errors," and *The Merchant of Venice*, are ascribed to "Shaxberd." *The Merry Wives of Windsor, Love's Labor's Lost*, and *Henry V* were also played, but, as with most of the plays listed, their author is not identified.

On May 20, 1609, one Thomas Thorpe was licensed to publish a volume of poems; when it appeared it was entitled simply *Shakespeares Sonnets*. Thorpe supplied a maddeningly knowing dedication, "To the only begetter of these ensuing sonnets Mr. W. H. all happiness and that eternity promised." Some sonnets had been circulating among a privileged group since before 1598, but we do not know the origin of Thorpe's copytext. When all speculation is stripped away we are obliged to admit that we do not know when or to whom the sonnets were written, or what the dedication means, and we have never identified any of the unnamed persons referred to in the poems. We do not even know whether the sonnets are correctly interpreted as revealing Shakespeare's life and self primarily or whether they deal principally with philosophical or literary conceits and conventions. If Sir Walter Raleigh could write one of the most passionate poems in the language to the cruel, bald, and rotten-toothed old queen who had flung him in prison, expressing his utter loyalty in terms of love melancholy, Shakespeare is entitled to be at least as sophisticated as he.

In 1608, the King's Men recovered the lease of the Blackfriars Theatre. It had been built by Richard Burbage's father, James, in 1596, when he had acquired the old priory where the boy players used to perform and converted it into an indoor theater. Unfortunately the residents' protests effectively prevented the company from ever using it. As winter quarters for the King's Men it was ideal, but as an intimate theater for a more select and sophisticated audience it required a different style of play, closer to the masques and pageants in which the court delighted. *Pericles, Prince of Tyre*, is obviously designed for the new conditions. In November 1611, *The Tempest* and *The Winter's Tale* were played before the king, who liked them well enough to have them revived for the celebrations which marked the marriage in 1613 of the Elector Palatine and Elizabeth Stuart, together with *Othello*, which the king had already seen at the Banqueting House at Whitehall in November 1604, "Sir John Falstaffe," *Julius Caesar*, and *Much Ado*.

Shakespeare was forty-eight, in the prime of life and at the zenith of his career, yet within months of that exhausting if triumphant season for the King's Servants we find him described as a resident of Stratford when he was called to London to give evidence in a civil action between Stephen Belott and his father-in-law, Christopher Mountjoy, in whose house Shakespeare had been a lodger in 1604. In 1613, he was paid 44 shilllings for designing the emblem and motto to be worn at the mock jousting on the king's accession day by the Earl of Rutland. He also bought the Blackfriars Gatehouse, apparently as an investment, to be managed by three nominees, his colleague John Heminges, William Johnson, and John Jackson.

On June 29, 1613, during a performance of *Henry VIII* at the Globe, a discharge of blanks set fire to the thatch and in less than an hour the playhouse had burned to the ground. Shakespeare took no part in the rebuilding and left no theater shares in his will. We do not know whether one of the King's Men risked his life to save the playbooks, or if they were kept somewhere else.

It is impossible to tell from the dating whether Shakespeare made his first will in January 1615 or 1616; he signed himself as the convention demanded, "in perfect health and memory." On March 25, 1616, he called his solicitor to draw up a second will to incorporate revisions made necessary by the marriage of Judith, his second daughter, to Thomas Quiney a month earlier. The document is characteristically terse and inscrutable. Ann Shakespeare is mentioned only in an afterthought written between the lines, "Item, I give unto my wife my second-best bed with all the furniture." As his widow, she was automatically entitled to one third of the estate; Shakespeare's laconic stipulation may have been his way of ensuring that in the division of his property, she kept the bed that they had always slept in. He remembers his colleagues, Burbage, Heminges, and Condell too, but only to the extent that he leaves them each 26 shillings 8 pence to buy mourning rings. Most of the will is devoted to the minute provisions he made for safeguarding the fortunes of his heiresses, as any responsible businessman would have done.

When and how he died we do not know. He was buried on Thursday, April 25, 1616. Tradition holds that he was born and died on the same day, April 23, St. George's Day.

Seven years passed before Heminges and Condell produced Shakespeare's noblest monument, the First Folio edition of thirty-six plays. They may have been spurred to it not only by the desire "to keep the memory of so worthy a friend and fellow alive" but also by William Jaggard's renewed attempt to exploit Shakespeare's popular reputation, for by

MR. WILLIAM

SHAKESPEARES

COMEDIES,
HISTORIES, &
TRAGEDIES.

Published according to the True Originall Copies.

LONDON
Printed by Isaac Iaggard, and Ed. Blount. 1623.

The title page of Shakespeare's First Folio includes this portrait by the engraver Martin Droeshout.

1619 he was again busied in the production of a series of pirated quartos under false names and dates.

The 1623 Folio is prefixed by only four commendatory poems. One, the panegyric by Ben Jonson, who "loved the man" and honored "his memory on this side idolatry as much as any," is justly famous. The others are mediocre offerings by obscure poets. Jonson's own Folio (1616) boasts more than three times as many, including verses by Shakespeare's friends and colleagues, Chapman and Beaumont. Six months after his death, Jonson was to be celebrated in a whole volume

This portrait of the British poet and playwright Ben Jonson (1572–1637) was painted around 1617 by Abraham van Blyenberch.

of eulogy, *Jonsonus Virbius*; in death, as in life, he was accounted the greater artist. However, from Jonson's own caveats we may infer that Shakespeare had a passionate following of his own, who revered him as a prodigy. On the one hand Jonson found himself irritably condemning Shakespeare's facility and on the other reminding the first bardolators that Shakespeare, like other poets, had to sweat "and strike the second heat / Upon the Muses' anvil."

Shakespeare's funerary monument at Holy Trinity Church in Stratford-upon-Avon, England, is usually attributed to Gheerart Janssen the Younger.

We know from the commendatory verse in the First Folio by Leonard Digges that Shakespeare's monument in Holy Trinity Church, Stratford, was already to be seen in 1623. Our knowledge of what Shakespeare looked like depends upon this likeness by Gheerart Janssen and the engraving by Martin Droeshout for the title page of the First Folio. In keeping with the rest of the evidence about Shakespeare the man, the portraits are both poorly realized and mutually incompatible. We do not know at whose instance the Stratford monument was raised, but we do know that in August 1623 that invisible woman Ann Shakespeare died and was buried alongside her husband in the chancel of Holy Trinity Church.

The purpose of recounting the bald and cryptic facts of Shakespeare's life shorn of the accretions of speculation which have busied throngs of scholars is simply to provide a fixed base for the discussion of Shakespeare's thought. His works have been ransacked time and again for evidence of his adherence to Catholicism, Puritanism, the Essex faction, Platonism, feminism, anti-feminism, and so forth, on the basis of different and incompatible assumptions about where he was at different times and on different occasions, and whom he knew. No such assumptions will be made in this slim volume, which is committed to a description of Shakespeare's thought as it is evinced in the works which he has left us.

Given the undeniable fact that Shakespeare seldom if ever spoke in his own person, a scrupulous discussion of his thought must take his invisibility into account as an aspect of his intellect. This is not to do what Shakespeare eulogists have so often done in praising him for having "in himself the germs of every faculty and feeling," although Shakespeare would probably have believed with Terence that, as he was human, nothing human should be alien to him. Hazlitt goes too far when he claims that Shakespeare could follow every human faculty and feeling "by anticipation, intuitively, into all their conceivable ramifications, through every change of fortune, or conflict of passion, or turn of thought." It may well be true that Shakespeare's perceptions were more comprehensive than those of more disciplined minds but they are not the products of intuition and Shakespeare is not merely the conduit of some kind of divine inspiration. Rather, he was profoundly aware of and interested in intellectual issues, which he did not choose to simplify, codify, reconcile, or resolve but rather to dramatize in such a way that his audience also became thrillingly aware of an extra dimension, an imaginative dimension, of daily life.

The chief pitfall threatening any discussion of Shakespeare's thought is the common assumption that the opinions of any character in a Shakespearean play are Shakespeare's own. Shakespeare was not a propagandist; he did not write plays as vehicles for his own ideas. Rather he developed a theater of dialectical conflict, in which idea is pitted against idea and from their friction a deeper understanding of the issues emerges. The resolution which is reached is not the negation of the conflict, but the stasis produced by art. Even as we applaud it, we recognize its fragility.

TWO

Poetics

●

THE VERY ARCHITECTURE OF SHAKESPEARE'S theater was emblematic. It was called after all the Globe, and its motto, "Totus mundus agit histrionem" (All the world's a stage), made a serious point. Well might Hamlet luxuriate in the reverberations of his double irony as he shows the audience all around and above and below him to Rosencrantz and Guildenstern: "This goodly frame the earth seems to me a sterile promontory, this most excellent canopy the air, look you, this brave o'erhanging firmament, this majestical roof fretted with golden fire, why it appeareth to me but a foul and pestilent congregation of vapors" (2.2.298–303).

The playhouses were known to be unhealthy places, which is why they were the first institutions to be closed down in times of plague; they were also the only places where all the denizens of London, from the

The Globe Theatre's distinctive architecture, seen in this undated wood engraving, allowed the audience to surround the players virtually on all sides.

meanest pickpocket to the grandest functionary, could foregather and actually experience their membership of a community. Even the largest churches did not afford the same spectacular possibilities, for the pulpit was raised above the congregation who stood all on one plane. In the theater the audience could see itself as a tapestry of faces, surging below in the pit and rising on the tiers around the wooden walls, with the actor on his promontory, the projecting stage, at their mercy.

The Playwrights' Defense of Their Art

The propaganda possibilities of the theater were enormous, as both secular and religious authorities were aware. In the early years of Elizabeth's reign players were tacitly encouraged to mount anti-Catholic entertainments, sometimes of quite scandalous and libelous intent, until the Crown deemed discretion to be the better part, the opportunities for Puritan propaganda outweighing the advantages of inciting anti-Catholic feeling. In Shakespeare's day the players' companies were forbidden to treat of religious matters. The placing of players under the protection of court dignitaries was not simply a way of protecting them from prosecution as rogues and mountebanks, but also of ensuring that the most effective propaganda weapon remained within control of the Crown. The religious reformers, deprived of access to this public platform, attacked it bitterly, and not without reason. The playhouses were disorderly places, where prostitutes went in search of clients for the bawdy houses that stood around. There were frequent brawls between the more irrepressible factions of apprentices and students, and other hotheads bearing arms. The Puritan corporation of the City of London had to pay the bill for both plague and riot, while competing unsuccessfully for the same population which, instead of devoting Sunday to godly exercises, flocked to the playhouses.

The Puritan attack on the stage was the best advertising the players' companies could have hoped for, but at the same time the playwrights were sensitive to the charges laid. It would never have occurred to any of them to deny that the theater had a responsibility to the public, which was not simply to entertain but to advance the common weal. This was to be done not by pious exhortation, but by devising an entertainment which presented moral teaching in a vivid, impressive, and memorable way. There was no Elizabethan playwright who had not cut his teeth on the Horatian maxim "Omne tulit punctum, qui miscuit utile dulci: Lectorem delectando pariterque monendo" (He has borne every point who has mingled the useful with the sweet, at the same time delighting and instructing the reader).

Hamlet's description of the players as the "abstract and brief chronicles of the time" is in part an answer and a challenge to the Puritans. Like the university men who wrote on the state of the public theaters, he betrays some impatience with the vapidity and vulgarity of much of what was staged, particularly by the Children of the Chapel, who performed at the indoor theater in Blackfriars for the amusement of those who could pay six times as much for their tickets as was asked at the Globe. There is nothing original or even surprising in Hamlet's claims for the theater, which could have been drawn from Shakespeare's own reading of Aristotle in any one of the Latin versions which proliferated in the sixteenth century or from any of the vernacular discussions of the issues raised by the *Poetics*, which most of his contemporaries interpreted in the light of their reading of Horace's *De Arte Poetica* and the commentaries on Cicero. Sir Philip Sidney's *Apologie for Poetry*, widely quoted long before its posthumous publication in 1595, is a fairly typical conflation of these sources, which provide Hamlet with his own version of Sidney's "true end of poetry," and the same contempt for "ridiculous excess."

> Suit the action to the word, the word to the action, with this special observance, that you o'erstep not the modesty of nature. For anything so o'erdone is from the purpose of playing, whose end, both at the first and now, was and is to hold as 'twere the mirror up to nature; to show virtue her feature, scorn her own image, and the very age and body of the time his form and pressure.

> *(3.2.17–24)*

Sir Philip Sidney (1554–86), the English poet, wrote in his *Apologie for Poetry* that "there is no Art delivered unto mankind that hath not the workes of nature for his principall object." Sidney appears in this 1577 portrait by an unknown English artist.

The edition of Terence which Shakespeare read at school would have been larded with commentary, "moralizing" every scene as if it had been a biblical parable. In fact, so accustomed were the intellectuals of his time to reading every kind of literature as if it were Christian parable that the works of the most cynical and amoral classical writers were seen as anxious enquiries into the meaning of life and the nature of the soul. Nor could Shakespeare have escaped learning the definition of comedy from the fourth-century grammarian Donatus, who attributed it to Cicero, among whose extant writings it has never been found. Comedy is "imitatio vitae, speculum consuetudinis, imago veritatis" (an imitation of life, a mirror of manners, an image of truth). The Christian interpretation of the definition involved the portrayal of the relation between God and man, of ways of behavior both ideal and reprehensible, and the demonstration of ethical issues.

In continental Europe, Renaissance drama existed in two distinct forms, and played to two separate audiences. The erudite theater, written in classical meters with highly formalized plotting, played to upper-class audiences or academics in private theaters and is in almost every surviving case deadly dull and stately. The popular theater was largely improvised along the lines of stock intrigues and stock characters studded with set pieces, songs, and dances for the display of the virtuosity of members of commercial troupes. Nowadays this kind of entertainment has acquired a kind of glamour based, one suspects, on a misunderstanding of the term *commedia dell'arte*, which simply means "professional theater." Italian *commedianti* visited England in the 1570s but their kind of entertainment did not catch on; plots based on adulterous intrigue were not likely to edify a population convulsed by religious antagonisms, especially when one of the tenderest areas involved the status of marriage.

Elizabethan popular drama was unique in Europe in that the playwrights insisted on absolute control. In the introduction to his verse translation (1610) of Thomas Tomkis's morality play, *Lingua*, Johannes Rhenanus described how such control was exercised.

> So far as actors are concerned they, as I noticed in England, are daily instructed, as it were in a school, so that even the most eminent actors have to allow themselves to be instructed by the dramatists,

which arrangement gives life and ornament to a well-written play, so that it is no wonder that the English players (I speak of the skilled ones) surpass and have the advantage of others.

Hamlet's speech to the players mirrors this exact situation. He has written at least part of the play they are about to perform and he gives precise instructions in the manner of delivery, "trippingly," not mouthing and grimacing or obscuring the matter with exaggerated gestures: "Let those that play your clowns speak no more than is set down for them" (3.2.38–39).

Richard Tarleton (1530–88) was not only Queen Elizabeth's favorite jester, he was also a skilled swordsman, musician, and writer. This image of Tarleton comes from a manuscript by the British calligrapher and schoolmaster John Scottowe (d. 1607), which was first published in facsimile in 1974.

Richard Tarleton, the queen's jester and star of the queen's players, was famous for extemporizing verse on themes suggested by the audience and for singing his own songs. After his death in 1588, his place as the funniest man in London was taken by William Kempe, who would have been the leading member of Lord Strange's company when Shakespeare was writing for them, and appears to have taken roles in performances of Shakespeare's plays.

The playwrights' domination of the theater was by no means a foregone conclusion, but something that they were obliged to defend with determination, as their audiences were quite likely to start laughing just as soon as the famous comics "peeped out" their heads. There would be little point in insisting upon such control if the purposes of playing were simply to entertain and to make money. The degree of seriousness of the playwright's expository intent is indicated by Hamlet's reason for wanting to control the clowns in the first place: "For there be of them that will themselves laugh, to set on some quantity of barren spectators to laugh too, though in the meantime some necessary question of the play be then to be considered" (3.2.40–43).

Shakespeare's "Honest Mirth"

The Puritan attack on the acting of plays rested on two assumptions, the first that the imitation of human speech and actions was lying and taught dissimulation, and the second that the dressing of men as women was evil in itself. Shakespeare mocks such ethical conundra in divers ways. In *Love's Labor's Lost* and *A Midsummer Night's Dream*, he goes behind the scenes to show the mounting of theatrical presentations, and deliberately poises the simplicity of the performers against the sophistication of the audience. Theseus's master of the revels warns the noble company (in *A*

Midsummer Night's Dream) that they will not enjoy the "tedious brief scene of young Pyramus / And his love Thisbe":

> It is not for you: I have heard it over,
> And it is nothing, nothing in the world;
> Unless you can find sport in their intents,
> Extremely stretch'd and conn'd with cruel pain
> To do you service.

(5.1.77–81)

Theseus's description of the importance of the active participation of the audience in creating and maintaining the illusion is a basic tenet of the Shakespearean aesthetic, to which he was to cling despite the gibes of more arrogant poets until the end of his writing career: "The best in this kind are but shadows; and the worst are no worse, if imagination amend them" (5.1.208–9).

The frantic efforts of the players to reassure their audience that there is no need to be afraid of Snug dressed up as a lion are seen in this context as ridiculous not only because the players are not so expert that they could deceive anybody, but because audiences know that what is being presented is invented. Indeed, the action is taken from a classical source that would be known to all literate people either from their school Latin or from Golding's translation, namely the *Metamorphoses* of Ovid.

In *Love's Labor's Lost*, the play is presented by a motley crew consisting of a fantastical Spanish braggart, perhaps descended from the Capitano of the *commedia dell'arte*, a pedant who might owe something of his characterization to the Bolognese doctor, a witty page,

Shakespeare may have patterned the character of Don Adriano de Armado in *Love's Labor's Lost* after a stock character from Roman comedy known as Miles Gloriosus, which Shakespeare would have known from childhood. This bas-relief of a Roman comedy scene can be seen in the Museo Archeologico Nazionale in Naples, Italy.

a curate, a constable, and a rustic. If they are types drawn from the popular stage of Europe, there is some irony in their undertaking to play an earnest and outdated popular Pageant of the Nine Worthies, the like of which could still be seen in English provincial towns. The contrast between the players and their play must have been deliberate. Well might the curate ask, "Where will you find men worthy enough to present them?" The curate's consciousness of his own unworthiness may be the reason that he dries completely so that the clown is obliged to speak in his defense: "There, an't shall please you: a foolish mild man; an honest man, look you, and soon dashed! He is a marvelous good neighbor, faith, and a very good bowler; but, for Alisander,—alas! you see how 'tis,—a little o'erparted" (5.2.575–79).

Costard's intervention not only scuttles whatever illusion the Pageant of the Nine Worthies has been able to build up, but also adds weight and depth to the illusion of the surrounding play world of Navarre. The defrocked actors seem as real as the audience, while the lords of Navarre and the ladies of France have become a kind of audience. When the figure of the envoy appears to announce the death of the king of France, even the Navarre world begins to slide. The lords, confusing dalliance with serious courtship, try to keep the play going, but the ladies have stepped outside it and become critics. Following the lead of the princess, who condemns Ferdinand of Navarre to real life, "frosts and fasts, hard lodging and thin weeds," Rosaline defines the proper use to which inventive talent should be put:

> You shall this twelve month term from day to day,
> Visit the speechless sick, and still converse
> With groaning wretches; and your task shall be
> With all the fierce endeavor of your wit
> To enforce the pained impotent to smile.
> BEROWNE: To move wild laughter in the throat of death?
> It cannot be; it is impossible:
> Mirth cannot move a soul in agony.
> ROSALINE: Why, that's the way to choke a gibing spirit,
> Whose influence is begot of that loose grace
> Which shallow laughing hearers give to fools.
> A jest's prosperity lies in the ear

Of him that hears it, never in the tongue
Of him that makes it: then, if sickly ears,
Deaf'd with the clamors of their own dear groans,
Will hear your idle scorns, continue then . . .

(5.2.842–57)

When those lines were first said in the theater, the audience knew that plague was abroad in the land. Within weeks the city fathers had closed the theaters in an effort to control the contagion. Rosaline's idea of the function of wit is peculiarly apposite, especially when we remember that the poorer members of Shakespeare's audience did not have the option of taking refuge in the country. The unspoken premise is that life is hard and painful, therefore delight has an ethical function in itself.

Shakespeare, unlike his better-educated competitors, flourished no whips and administered no pills. He was well aware that there were other kinds of plays which carped and moaned at an audience which was too ignorant to appreciate lofty themes and cultured discourse, but he made no attempt (unless it be in *Troilus and Cressida*) to imitate the satiric vein. In *A Midsummer Night's Dream*, such a play, "The Thrice Three Muses mourning for the Death of Learning, late deceas'd in Beggary," is rejected by Theseus, who comments merely,

That is some satire, keen and critical,
Not sorting with a nuptial ceremony.

(5.1.54–55)

It took John Davies of Hereford in *The Scourge of Folly* (1621) to extend to Shakespeare the title that he should have had by common consent.

To our English Terence, Mr. Will. Shakespeare

Some say (good Will) which I, in sport, do sing,

Hadst thou not played some kingly parts in sport,

Thou hadst been companion for a king;

And, been a king among the meaner sort.

Some others rail; but, rail as they think fit,

Thou hast no railing, but, a reigning wit:

> And honesty thou sow'st, which they do reap,

> So, to increase their stock which they do keep.

This rather handsome little compliment has been taken as evidence that Shakespeare usually took the part of the king when he acted. The *jeu d'esprit* turns upon kingliness, and ought not to be interpreted too literally. What is important to the discussion is the distinction Davies makes between satire and honest mirth. Shakespeare's is the comedy not of "loud laughing" but of "soft smiling."

Knowing nothing more commendable for a mans recreation

Than Mirth which is used in an honest fashion.

The Tempest: Poetics in Action

The nearest thing to a systematic exposition of Shakespeare's poetic is *The Tempest*, the play chosen by Heminges and Condell to head the First Folio, in an exceptionally clear and carefully edited version. The plot is wholly original and clearly artificial; the least enquiring audience must be aware that the play's concerns are metaphysical. There is a consensus that *The Tempest* deals with the beloved Renaissance debate

"Nature versus Art"; what is not so often discerned is that Shakespeare's nature and art are a continuum. *The Tempest* deals with good and bad art, useful and noxious, and takes an original position in conscious opposition to the schoolmen.

The play begins with a display of the kind of gimmickry ridiculed by Jonson, when a "roll'd bullet is heard to say It thunders" and "tempestuous drum rumbles." The unusually elaborate stage directions ask for "a tempestuous noise of thunder and lightning," which no sooner produced is found to be Prospero's doing:

> If by your Art, my dearest father, you have
> Put the wild waters in this roar, allay them.

(1.2.1–2)

The manipulation of the audience's cooperation is intricate: they are asked to consent to the mechanical noises being real weather, and then to the idea that a character on stage, in some supernatural way, has caused them. Miranda is an innocent; Prospero has to reassure her by telling her what the adults in the audience already know, that there's no harm done. Laying aside his magic garment, he becomes chorus to the play and provides a synopsis of events leading up to the play time. He has been a temporal ruler whose kingdom has been usurped, because he dedicated himself to "closeness and the bettering of his mind." He admits no guilt but his language raises the question at several points. His "library was dukedom large enough," and here on the island he has, besides "rich garments, linen stuffs and necessaries," volumes that he prizes "above" his dukedom. The island, like the stage itself, has two principal resources, costume and script.

Then Prospero puts Miranda, a figure of the spectator, to sleep while he calls upon his instrument, Ariel, described in the dramatis personae simply as "an airy spirit." The scene might be compared to Oberon's commanding of Puck, but there is a most important difference. Where Puck is a willing instrument, Ariel is reluctant, yearning

The action of *The Tempest* begins on board
a ship, during what the audience at first
believes is a fierce storm—a scene depicted
in this 1797 engraving after a painting by
George Romney (1734–1802). The engraving
and painting were commissioned by John
Boydell, a renowned British publisher
and engraver, who with his nephew Josiah
established the Boydell Shakespeare Gallery
in London, a massive endeavor that aimed
to exhibit a comprehensive collection of
British-made Shakespearean paintings, some
of which were later engraved for publication.
The building of Boydell's gallery and the
commissioning of hundreds of paintings was
both symptomatic of and instrumental in the
building of Shakespeare's reputation as "not
for an age but for all time." Between 1760 and
1900, more than two thousand pictures of
Shakespeare subjects were hung in the annual
exhibitions the Royal Academy, more than a
fifth of the total.

for his manumission. It may be more profitable to think of him not as
some aspect of Prospero's mind or soul, especially when doing so cannot
make much sense of the elaborate history of Ariel's life before Prospero came to the island, when he was imprisoned by Caliban's witch
mother in a cloven pine, but as the power of the collective imagination,

playwright's words working on audience's faculty. The personification would then be directly descended from the image of winged thought used by the Chorus in *Henry V*:

> Thus with imagin'd wing our swift scene flies
> In motion of no less celerity
> Than that of thought.

(3, Chorus, 1–3)

If Prospero's island is the stage, which in one sense at least it surely is, then it does pass from ruler to ruler, most of whom will make no use of the prodigious figurative power of the poetic drama. Moreover, this power can only be exercised in the theater; when Prospero leaves his island, he loses Ariel as well. He also loses Miranda. However complex such ideas may seem, they are child's play to that section of Shakespeare's

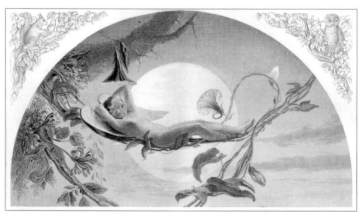

This fanciful interpretation of Ariel, the "airy spirit" from *The Tempest*, was engraved by C. W. Sharpe (1818–99) after a painting by H. J. Townsend. Note that Ariel is depicted as female.

audience which grew up on emblems and *imprese*, and habitually thought in personifications. There is no single right reading of the complex allegory of *The Tempest*, for Shakespeare becomes involved in the polarities presented by his characters and develops many resonances in them beyond the possibility of a single thesis. Ariel is air and Caliban earth; Ariel soul and Caliban body; Ariel intellect and Caliban appetite; Ariel intellection and Caliban sensory response—and so on. Prospero loves the one, indeed, addresses him much more fondly than he ever does his daughter, and despises the other. It is Prospero's tragedy that he must dote on Ariel, whom he must lose, and despise Caliban, the thing of darkness he is forced at the end of the play to acknowledge as his.

It may well be true that Shakespeare put together his Caliban out of his reading of voyage literature, especially the Bermuda pamphlets, and that his name is some sort of corruption of "Caribbean"; it seems equally plausible that he was influenced by his reading of Montaigne's essay "Of the Caniballes" in Florio's translation, especially as Caliban's name is an anagram of can[n]ibal. Shakespeare may have shared Montaigne's compassion for savages, for he makes it clear that if Caliban is barbarous he is also barbarously treated by Prospero, who has condemned him to brutish toil and keeps him at it by torturing him with cramps, side stitches, and bone aches, in much the same way that those who enslaved the Brazilian Indians forced them to work every day without pay by the use of the bludgeon. The laboring poor of Shakespeare's London, deformed by drudgery, illness, and accident, tormented by vermin, illiterate and unregenerate, must have presented a certain Calibanesque aspect. The public duty of the playwright was to bring the caviar of his angelic intellectual exercise within the grasp of these savage hordes, who were quite capable of disrupting performances which they could not follow.

By the time he wrote *The Tempest* (ca. 1611) Shakespeare had lived to see the decline of the theater of daylight, which could play only during a limited summer season, and the gradual ascendancy of the indoor theater, the theater of lamplight, which could play to smaller houses, charge higher prices, and present plays all the year round. The influence of the indoor theaters began to affect what was offered in the open theaters. The fervor of didacticism weakened and the exercise of imagination became less important, as the audience was regaled by pageants and spectacles following the lead set by the royal patrons. Theater became less serious and more sensational; the great national concerns gave way to domestic intrigue; the smell of cowslips and violets to musk and civet, if not in reality then in the imagery of the plays.

While the noisy groundlings tyrannized over the public theater, the coterie theater found itself in the situation of having to gratify the vanity of its most powerful patrons, who could decide what should be played and when, and what themes should be treated in new works and how. The persona of Sonnet LXXVI ironically laments his inability to change with the times:

Why is my verse so barren of new pride?
So far from variation or quick change?
Why, with the time, do I not glance aside
To new-found methods, and to compounds strange?
Why write I still all one, ever the same,
And keep invention in a noted weed,
That every word doth almost tell my name,
Showing their birth, and where they did proceed?

The mock lament is actually a boast of truth and constancy, as the change of tone in the last line shows. Shakespeare has left us a satiric portrait of the poet who writes verses by the yard to please a patron in *Timon of Athens* (1607–8). He is a curious, chameleon figure, and the point of Shakespeare's ridicule of his affectation and frivolous self-interest can be seen as of a piece with the contemptuous dismissal of coterie theater in *Hamlet*, as "little eyases, that cry out on the top of the question and are most tyrannically clapp'd for it." The persona of the sonnets makes an inverted boast of his failure as a courtier, yet, after he had dedicated himself to the popular stage, Shakespeare found himself, as leading writer for the King's Men, a court poet after all. It is not far-fetched to conclude that he actually preferred to serve an unlettered, needy, impressionable public with the stuff of magnificent myth, rather than study the whims of educated, aristocratic taste. In *Cymbeline*, for example, true British nobility is nurtured far from the debased court; Belarius's animadversions can be construed to apply to the two kinds of theater, of daylight and of lamplight:

> Stoop, boys: this gate
> Instructs you how t'adore the heavens; and bows you
> To a morning's holy office. The gates of monarchs
> Are arch'd so high that giants may jet through
> And keep their impious turbans on, without
> Good morrow to the sun.

> *(3.3.2–7)*

Certainly for most of his career, and perhaps for all of it, Shakespeare cast his lot primarily with the theater of daylight, yet he could not conclude that in doing so he had actually aided the moral improvement of his audience. By 1611, the steady deterioration of public morality in England, and the increase in social tension and factionalism, were obvious to less perceptive observers than Shakespeare. The audiences he had found in the 1590s had disintegrated. *The Tempest* may be in typically oblique Shakespearean fashion a salute to the groundlings. Of all the inhabitants of the isle none appreciates what Prospero and Ariel create more than Caliban.

> the isle is full of noises,
> Sounds and sweet airs, that give delight, and hurt not.
> Sometimes a thousand twangling instruments
> Will hum about mine ears; and sometime voices,
> That, if I had then wak'd after long sleep,
> Will make me sleep again: and then, in dreaming,
> The clouds methought would open, and show riches
> Ready to drop upon me; that, when I wak'd,
> I cried to dream again.

(3.2.133–41)

Shakespeare had often referred to his own dramaturgy as the making of dreams, most obviously in *Midsummer Night's Dream*. In the Epilogue, Puck sums up the dream imagery that has been woven through the play:

> If we shadows have offended,
> Think but this, and all is mended,
> That you have but slumber'd here

While these visions did appear.
And this weak and idle theme,
No more yielding, but a dream . . .

(5.1.409–14)

Like *The Tempest*, *A Midsummer Night's Dream* has elements of the psychomachia, or battle within the soul, as its main characters are tormented by delusions, dreams within the dream, but whereas the source of their suffering is fancy or imagination, and Shakespeare's theme primarily the interaction of poetry and imagination, in *The Tempest* we are concerned much more with the making of shows, the counterfeiting of actions, the creative artist as illusionist. The conclusion of *A Midsummer Night's Dream*, for all its deference and mock humility, is optimistic: ritual tames the imagination of lovers and poets.

Like Ariel, the character of Puck, from *A Midsummer Night's Dream*, is a spirit. This image of Puck and a group of his fellow spirits was painted by Richard Dadd in 1841.

> . . . all the story of the night told over,
>
> And all their minds transfigur'd so together,
>
> More witnesseth than fancy's images,
>
> And grows to something of great constancy . . .

(5.1.23–26)

Caliban dreams of his own happy ending, his salvation, expressed in the common image of a stored-up treasure, of grace accumulated during his life of toil. His vision shows that he has imagination—stimulated, all unbeknown to Prospero, by Prospero's art—and, by the use of it, he may transcend his brutish condition. Besides all the other things he is, Caliban is a figure of the crowd drawn into the theater by the simple desire of the *dulce* of pastime, of "pleasant mirth," recreation and temporary freedom from drudgery and pain. He is the sensuous conduit through which the dramatist's art is made flesh. He has much in common with Miranda who is totally without art and ripe for exploitation. If she is debauched by the scenes and characters Prospero exposes her to, he must bear the guilt of her defilement.

As a character Prospero is not entirely sympathetically presented. His stage-managing of the meeting of Ferdinand and Miranda is half contemptuous. By way of making Miranda a more valued acquisition he can think of no alternative to treating Ferdinand as he treats Caliban, lying and feigning to justify such treatment, while congratulating himself in asides, which never allow the audience to forget that he is the contriver of all that they see. Old Gonzalo's idea of an Arcadian society established on the island is a curious comment on the autocracy that Prospero has established by the free use of fear, mystification, and torture. It is Prospero who puts the Neapolitans to sleep so that Sebastian and Antonio can plot against the life of the king and that he can send Ariel to foil them.

It is the more surprising then that two characters can arrive on the island without Prospero's prior knowledge.

It has been noticed by Katharine M. Lea among others that the antics of Stephano and Trinculo belong to the stock of *lazzi* or comic routines of the *commedia dell'arte*; what is not usually remarked is the contrast between these scenes and the rest of the play. They are the most entertaining, especially if the players follow the lead of the *commedianti dell'arte* and combine their comic lines with tumbling and ludicrous contortions of face and body, but the two buffoons also make disturbing references to crude and stupid spectacles, which were enormously successful. People "who will not give a doit to relieve a lame beggar, will lay out ten to see a dead Indian." They give Caliban wine as their way of gaining control over him, and he finds it superior magic to the dreams provoked by Prospero, imagining that these two slavers are leading him to freedom. There is now a new motif in the play; Prospero will have to compete with these interlopers for ownership of Caliban. The theme of usurpation, doubled in Sebastian and Antonio's plot against the king of Naples, is strangely paralleled by the zanies' conquest of Caliban, with the significant difference that Prospero, intent on stage-managing the show for his daughter's betrothal, is oblivious of his slave's impending revolt. When he remembers, he loses control of the shared illusion with its cast of reapers and nymphs; "with a strange, hollow and confused noise, they heavily vanish." Then Prospero utters his apologia.

> Our revels now are ended. These our actors,
> As I foretold you, were all spirits, and

Are melted into air, into thin air:
And, like the baseless fabric of this vision,
The cloud-capp'd towers, the gorgeous palaces,
The solemn temples, the great globe itself,
Yea, all which it inherit, shall dissolve,
And, like this insubstantial pageant faded,
Leave not a rack behind. We are such stuff
As dreams are made on; and our little life
Is rounded with a sleep.

(4.1.148–58)

This is the most moving of all the statements of the commonplace Elizabethan parallel between the theater and the created universe. The equation of human life with a transitory show struck Shakespeare's contemporaries as irresistibly true, whether they were Platonists, Stoics, skeptics, or Christians. Indeed, Elizabethans were often all four.

Before he can rest, Prospero must deal with the people who have seduced Caliban. Already the audience's view of Caliban is becoming independent of Prospero's assessment of him, as they have seen him in situations of which Prospero has known nothing. They have realized that he too has innocence, when they saw him making obeisance to a drunken buffoon. His passionate yearning for freedom is only too understandable, but we understand just as well that he will never find it. Prospero devises a show of tinsel finery to sidetrack the vulgarians, but he is not present to see Caliban's disillusionment, or his vehement contempt. Caliban emerges as superior to these worldlings, but Prospero sends his bandogs after him notwithstanding. It takes Ariel, impervious to human emotion as he is, to teach Prospero that "the rarer action is in virtue than in vengeance." He is forced to realize that his exercise of art has not been disinterested.

Prospero's résumé of his powers includes some that we have not seen, in this play at any rate:

> . . . graves at my command
> Have wak'd their sleepers, op'd, and let 'em forth
> By my so potent Art.

(5.1.48–50)

Such a claim seems truer of Shakespeare himself than of Prospero, and the "rough magic" that must be abjured could well be the kind of dramaturgy ridiculed by Ben Jonson, where the poet invokes huge tracts of space and time and spectacular events, with nothing to aid his painting with language but a battery of crude sound effects and the imagination of his hearers. History was on Jonson's side; the theater of the seventeenth century withdrew into a narrower compass, observed the unities, mocked at the shapeless inclusiveness of earlier art. Dryden was too good a critic not to know that Shakespeare was the greater artist: "All images of nature were still present to him, and he drew them not laboriously, but luckily; when he describes anything, you more than see it, you feel it too." Nevertheless, Dryden followed the example of Jonson, finding in him the kind of correctness and orthodoxy that permits imitation. He did not dare to attempt to unleash the collective imagination so that it could traverse the oceans and telescope the lifetime of a man into an hour or two or hold converse with ghosts and fairies. Part of the explanation for Shakespeare's lack of influence on British dramaturgy, which stands in total contrast with his utter pervasiveness in the language, is to be found in the fact that the Elizabethan audience, hungry, responsive, unselfconscious as it was, did not outlive the old queen.

The Epilogue to *The Tempest* has been derided as doggerel, literally interpreted as Shakespeare's farewell to the stage, and supposed to be an interpolation by another hand. It is written in rhymed tetrameters, the most artless of English meters and quite unlike the majestic blank verse of Prospero the magician.

> Now my charms are all o'erthrown,
> And what strength I have's mine own,
> Which is most faint: now, 'tis true,
> I must be here confin'd by you,
> Or sent to Naples. Let me not,
> Since I have my dukedom got,
> And pardon'd the deceiver, dwell
> In this bare island by your spell;
> But release me from my bands
> With the help of your good hands:
> Gentle breath of yours my sails
> Must fill, or else my project fails,
> Which was to please. Now I want
> Spirits to enforce, Art to enchant;
> And my ending is despair,
> Unless I be reliev'd by prayer,
> Which pierces so, that it assaults
> Mercy itself, and frees all faults.
>> As you from crimes would pardon'd be,
>> Let your indulgence set me free.

Prospero is now so feeble that he cannot get himself off the stage. The tetrameters are made to halt, by placing the strongest syntactical and rhetorical pauses within the short lines, while the strong rhymes chime out the line endings. His helplessness could not be more remorselessly conveyed. Neither Prospero nor Shakespeare is so much bidding farewell to the stage as begging to be released from it and pardoned for any evil done during his reign. The grandeur of this act of utter humility is staggering; the vein of anxiety running through the

John Dryden (1631–1700), depicted in this portrait by an unknown artist, was a poet and literary critic who was a fervent admirer of Shakespeare. This portrait is usually dated 1664, which makes it the earliest known likeness of Dryden.

play, about the roughness of the magic, the fragility of innocence, the godlike power of the creators of illusory worlds, the irresistible tendency of man to debauchery rather than improvement, the blindness and self-indulgence of intellectuals, has cropped out, as the defrocked hierophant begs our intercession to save his soul.

Shakespeare and the World of the Play

There is more to *The Tempest* than an exploration of aesthetics or dramaturgy, and there is more to Shakespeare's poetics than can appear in such a brief discussion. He was, like all his contemporaries, intensely aware of genre or kinds of drama, and equally aware that what he was creating was a curious mixture of kinds. His characters frequently comment on the play that they are in, for example, Berowne in *Love's Labor's Lost*:

> Our wooing doth not end like an old play;
> Jack hath not Jill: these ladies' courtesy
> Might well have made our sport a comedy.

(5.2.866–88)

He knew too that educated opinion considered his disregard of the unities of time and place to be a flaw, but he doggedly persisted in creating vast actions and invoking the imagery of landscape rather than the closets and street doors of baroque theater. Behind this variety was a unity of purpose which strengthened Shakespeare in resisting the pressure from his contemporaries to conform to pseudo-classical ideals. His own use of classic five-act structure shows that he understood the aesthetic principles underlying city comedy and Senecan tragedy. *The Comedy of Errors* uses the Plautine stage with its three street doors, restricts its action to the "scene individable" and to a single day. *The Merry Wives of Windsor* is an impeccable example of city comedy and *Julius Caesar* is probably the chastest and most symmetrical example of classical tragedy in English. Unity of tone, harmony, and compactness never became for Shakespeare ends in themselves; he was more concerned to open up the possibilities afforded by his sources than to lock them into any expository form. While it is possible to trace many typical Elizabethan preoccupations through Shakespeare's *œuvre*, it is impossible to decide categorically what he thought about the rights and duties of kings, nobles, and commoners, or the fortunes of war or religious faction or any of the notions upon which his contemporaries disagreed with increasing bitterness as the inexorable progress toward civil war gathered momentum. Shakespeare is typical of what was best in the tradition of heroic Protestantism in that he sought above all to discredit the idea of lip service. In his theatrical teaching he did not aim at agreement with a position already taken but at understanding of what was involved in the issue. Thus his theater does not attempt to dazzle or overwhelm the individual sensibility, but to stimulate it to new insights and sympathies. The proper instrument for this stimulation was language, and in particular language in performance.

The medium and the message coincide in Shakespeare's work at many points. It is not easy for us now to grasp how central the image of theater was to the Elizabethan *Weltanschauung*. Obviously an illiterate population has to absorb information through representation; all holders of rank, all professions, all trades were designated by their attributes and acted in accordance with the expectations of their social rank. The queen on her throne, or on her horse at Tilbury, the heretics and rebels on the scaffold, the priests in their pulpits, and the criers of their wares all knew that their success was dependent on the quality of their performance, be it success in moving hearts, in altering settled opinion, or in selling live shellfish. Shakespeare took this numinous reality and orchestrated its many modes so that in "all their minds," the players', the poet's, and the multifarious throng of listeners', "transfigur'd so together," his work would bear witness to something more permanent than opinion, and "grow to something of great constancy."

> A dream is all wrong, absurd, composite, and yet at the same time it is completely right . . . if Shakespeare is great, his greatness is displayed only in the whole *corpus* of his plays, which create their

This drawing of the Swan Theatre—a copy by Arend van Buchell of an original by his friend Johannes de Witt, who visited London in 1596—is the only known extant drawing of the interior of an Elizabethan public theater. According to de Witt, the theater had a capacity of three thousand people. The sketch was discovered in the Utrecht University Library in 1880.

own language and world. In other words he is completely unrealistic. (Like a dream.)

Wittgenstein's contemporaries might have thought that he had simply failed to understand Shakespeare, but nowadays we are beginning to use this kind of thinking as a starting point for an exploration of his mode of thought, far more relevant to us in its dynamic than in its conclusions. Indeed, it might be said that the strength of Shakespeare's position is that he refrains from coming to conclusions but leaves that to those who complete his utterance, the audience and the actors in the theater.

Changling

Simpleton

S^r I Falstafe

Hostes

Clause

THREE

Ethics

●

Shakespeare's Concept of Personality

It was not essential to have studied Plato in order to believe and feel that what was real about human beings was not how they looked or dressed, or how they spoke and what they said, but resided in what was eternal and indestructible about them, their souls. The soul was not simply a static entity, like an invisible identity card, but a dynamic principle, the fire breathed by God into the clay. Just as the actor animated different trappings in different situations in the same play, and in different plays at different times, the soul animated the protean body through all its changes. One way a modern mind could grasp

This frontispiece is found in *The Wits, or, sport upon sport*, a collection of drolls (short comic scenes) supposedly compiled by Francis Kirkman and published by Henry Marsh in 1662. The collection contained three drolls from Shakespeare, including scenes featuring Falstaff entitled "The Bouncing Knight."

What is our life? A play of passion
Our mirth the music of division;
Our mothers' wombs the tiring houses be,
Where we are dressed for this short comedy;
Heaven the judicious sharp spectator is
That sits and marks who doth act amiss;
Our graves that hide us from the searching sun
Are like drawn curtains when the play is done.
Thus march we playing to our latest rest—
Only we die in earnest, that's no jest.

(Sir Walter Raleigh)

Sir Walter Raleigh (1552–1618), the famed British poet, soldier, and explorer, is depicted in this 1588 portrait attributed to an artist known as H.

· · · · ·

the relationship is to think of the genotype, the human being in terms of his genetic potential for development, in relation to the phenotype, the pallid and partial realization of that staggering capability. The wastage of human potential in infant death, devastating illness, lack of opportunity for intellectual development, together with war, plague, and famine, was far more strikingly obvious to Elizabethans than it is to us, and their need to believe that life was merely a fleshly interlude marring the eternal life of the soul was so much greater. It helped to bear the unbearable if one could say with Antonio in *The Merchant of Venice*:

> I hold the world but as the world Gratiano,
> A stage, where every man must play a part,
> And mine a sad one.

(1.1.77–79)

In Raleigh's little poem (opposite) there is no doubt that the player outlives his roles, just as the actor outlives the three hours' traffic of the stage. For Macbeth, who wants to kill his soul, the player disappears once he leaves the stage:

> Life's but a walking shadow; a poor player,
> That struts and frets his hour upon the stage,
> And then is heard no more . . .

(5.5.24–26)

The Shakespearean concept of character is dependent upon the vivid apprehension of the unreality of life compared to eternity. His characters are not defined by their actions nor are their personalities rigid constructs which control their capacity for action. His personages are not involved in a search for identity, but search for ways to transcend that identity, which is transitory, and free the spirit, which is made in God's likeness, eternal and immutable. One of the ways of freeing the spirit from the trammels of its earthly role is to replace the fleshly mask with another, the mask of art, which more faithfully portrays the soul beneath. The feigned image of poetry speaks directly to the apprehension of the soul.

It follows, then, that the Elizabethan dramatist is concerned less to present us with characters who are unique or remarkable for their eccentricity or quiddity than with convincing renditions of types. It was not sufficient to label the type and set it about its business on the stage, although many Elizabethan interlude writers did just that. The playwright was required to have a deep understanding of the way such representative characters behaved and of how they came to be what they were, so that the audience could feel that there but for the grace of God went they—or conversely, in the case of virtue, that they too might aspire to the same distinction. In his *Apologie for Poetry* Sir Philip Sidney writes:

> See whether wisdom and temperance in Ulysses and Diomedes, valor in Achilles, friendship in Nisus and Euryalus, even to an ignorant man carry not an apparent shining, and, contrarily, the remorse of conscience in Oedipus, the soon repenting pride of Agamemnon, the self-devouring cruelty in his father Atreus, the violence of ambition in the two Theban brothers, the sour-sweetness of revenge in Medea, and, to fall lower, the Terentian Gnatho and our Chaucer's pandar so expressed that we now use their names to

signify their trades; and finally, all virtues, vices, and passions so in their natural seats laid to the view that we seem not to hear of them, but clearly to see through them . . .

To carry out "the purpose of playing, whose end both at the first and now, is to hold as 'twere the mirror up to nature; to show virtue her feature, scorn her own image," a company needed, beside him "who plays the king," an adventurous knight, a lover, a humorous man, a clown, and a lady—the six players who formed the personnel of the traveling troupes. Between them they would have had to take all the parts in the repertory, doubling and trebling where necessary, and so subtly under-lining the protean nature of the individual himself. Jaques in *As You Like It* gives a fuller description of the parts played by one man in the course of a lifetime:

> All the world's a stage,
> And all the men and women merely players.
> They have their exits and their entrances,
> And one man in his time plays many parts,
> His acts being seven ages.

(2.7.139–43)

In his description of the seven ages, Jaques provides us with a series of little character sketches, all self-contained, each stage apparently deriving nothing from the age before. In this world human beings pass through rites of passage; they graduate from school and become amo-rous poets, qualify for knight service at twenty-one and become soldiers, marry and turn businessmen, see their children married, decline into

This late-nineteenth-century lithograph, after a painting by Robert Smirke (1752–1845), depicts the sixth of the seven ages of man, as enumerated by Jaques in act 2, scene 7, of *As You Like It*. Smirke painted twenty-six pictures for the Boydell Shakespeare Gallery (see page 41), including one for each of the seven ages of man.

senility, and die. At each stage, they play stock roles: the lover pants, sighs, and turns sonnets, the soldier huffs and puffs, the justice pontificates.

Jaques gives to one part the name "pantaloon," from one of the characters of the *commedia dell'arte*. The other parts could be cast from the same repertoire, as Harlequin, *il Capitano*, *il dottore*, and *il vecchio*, and we could find a similar spectrum in the *commedia erudita* and the Roman comedy from which it derives. The word "theater" in Shakespeare's time meant not principally a place where one might watch dramas, or even a place where actions are played out (as in the modern survivals *operating theater* and *theater of war*), but something further, implying a whole gamut displayed. Theater in this sense did not present actions of particular men in particular places, but a picture of man's life *in toto*. This was the claim which lay behind the calling of the playhouse built in Shoreditch in 1576 "The Theatre." Gradually the name lost its connotation of universality to become for us typified by the narrow world of limelight and greasepaint. Long before Shakespeare's death the playwrights had lost confidence in their power to offer a "conspectus" or compendious view.

It is important to remember in considering Elizabethan theater that the search for truth was still conducted in the universities by public disputation rather than by experimentation behind closed doors. The empirical method was inextricably confused with the disreputable practice of alchemy. Schoolmen struggled to prove the most intractable matters—such as whether or not there was more than one world—by debating before an audience, using the full repertory of rhetorical devices. We ought not to be surprised when Hamlet refers to "some necessary question of the play." As a schools man himself, Hamlet would treat any play as argument, seeking out the meaning adumbrated by the combination of speeches, actions, and characters. The play he chooses to show the king is the crudest kind of allegory, a sort of dramatized *roman-à-clef*, but it does demonstrate in an elementary way how the feigned action of the drama is meant to illuminate the unsynthesized manifold of everyday life. It follows, then, that the meaning of Shakespearean plays cannot be expressed as functions of the individuality of the characters, for this is to deny their exemplary function and to interpose a third wall between them and the audience—yet in performance, by analogy with cinema and the way character is developed in novels, this is often done.

The Nature of Evil: *Othello*

In Shakespearean tragedy there is always an element of psychomachia, or the struggle within the soul, which may be externalized in many ways. One of the simplest, that Shakespeare would have taken over from the morality plays, is to show evil working on the protagonist in the person of a Vice. The Vice may be a lineal descendant of the intriguing servant of classical comedy or he may be a less self-conscious, more homegrown product. It is futile to demand motivation from the Vice, or reasons for his actions, for the point about evil is that it is absurd, unmotivated, and inconsistent. Such a character is Iago, whom generations of critics have struggled to psychoanalyze without success. His one object is to destroy Othello and he can have no good reason for it. Elizabethan audiences would have recognized Iago with his strange lopsided black humor, his chaotic and mildly hysterical motivation, and his parasitic relationship to Othello, even if he had not tacitly accepted Brabantio's identification:

> BRABANTIO: Thou art a villain.
>
> IAGO: You are a senator.

> *(1.1.118)*

To be sure there is more in the delineation of Iago than, say, in that of the witches in *Macbeth*, for Shakespeare is at pains to show how a certain kind of evil, common enough in truth, is apt to manifest itself. In case we should forget that Iago is the tempter, he reminds us, telling us that he hates Othello as he hates "hell's pains," prophesying: "There are many events in the womb of time, which will be delivered" (1.3.369–70); "Hell and night / Must bring this monstrous birth to the world's light" (1.3.401–2).

In this scene from a 1943 production of *Othello*, Paul Robeson plays the title role opposite Jose Ferrer's Iago. The production, in which Uta Hagen assumed the role of Desdemona, played at the Shubert Theater on Broadway for nine months. The *New York Times* critic said: "Mr. Ferrer follows the track that Iago is unexplained evil . . . his Iago is a sort of half dancing, half strutting Mephistopheles."

Iago's ubiquity in the play as he skips from character to character, organizing the complicated scenario which will entrap Othello, is more than natural, as is his mad inventiveness in luring Rodrigo and Cassio to their doom. To seduce Cassio he becomes the Morality character Good Fellowship, suddenly bursting into a wassail song. Cassio thinks that the devil who plays on him is wine, but Iago knows better. "Come, come, good wine is a good familiar creature" (2.3.300).

Chortling over his own equivocations, he explains himself at length:

And what's he then, that says I play the villain,
When this advice is free I give, and honest . . .

(2.3.327–28)

> Divinity of hell!
> When devils will their blackest sins put on,
> They do suggest at first with heavenly shows,
> As I do now . . .

(2.3.341–44)

The irony is wrung higher and higher as Othello, by wit not witchcraft, is drawn into Iago's plot.

> EMILIA: I will be hang'd, if some eternal villain,
> Some busy and insinuating rogue,
> Some cogging cozening slave, to get some office,
> Have not devis'd this slander; I'll be hang'd else.
> IAGO: Fie! there is no such man; it is impossible.

(4.2.132–36)

It is difficult to imagine how Iago's line can be said without a sly look, a nod or a wink to the audience, especially as the Vice is traditionally a comic character, a Merrygreek.

As only the audience and none of the actors except Iago know the extent of his machinations, a kind of complicity has developed between them. Those critics who might lament the relationship between Iago and the schema of the Vice might be mollified by realization of the immense subtlety of drawing the audience into complicity in the hounding of the alien to self-destruction. For much of the action the audience is required to believe that the stage is dark. All the characters except Iago are hoodwinked by darkness, while Iago, like the Black Dog of Edmonton, scurries round them, egging them on to murder. When Othello learns the part that Iago has played, he interprets it correctly (5.2.287–88):

> I look down towards his feet, but that's a fable,
> If that thou be'st a devil, I cannot kill thee.

And Iago taunts him: "I bleed, sir, but not kill'd" (5.2.289). Othello begs for a reason why Iago has "ensnared" his "soul and body," but, his work done, the Vice has no further function: "Demand me nothing, what you know, you know, / From this time forth I never will speak word" (5.2.304–5).

Because Iago's behavior cannot be explained in terms of personality, but rather in terms of a force, "More fell than anguish, hunger, or the sea" (5.2.363), the action of *Othello* opens out to include the audience, and their perception of the struggle of good and evil. They do not go home hoping they will never meet an Iago, but rather understanding something of the nature of evil and how soon bright things come to confusion. The ethical notion of evil as defective, absurd, and inconsistent is Aristotelian, but the embodiment of these characteristics in an agent, which makes possible the dynamic presentation of evil as an active force, is Christian. We no longer feel, as Shakespeare's contemporaries did, the ubiquity of Satan, but Iago is still serviceable to us, as an objective correlative of the mindless inventiveness of racist aggression. Iago is still alive and kicking and filling migrants' letterboxes with excrement.

The Capacity for Change: *Henry V*

If the premise upon which the poets built their justification of their profession is that theater is one means by which citizens are taught to shun

King Henry V of England,
depicted in this portrait by
an unidentified English artist
of the late sixteenth or early
seventeenth century, reigned
from 1413 until his death
in 1422.

evil and pursue the good, it follows that reformation and redemption must be possible. As we have seen from Jaques's précis of human life, Elizabethans did not regard personality as a given, limiting human capability. Where the novel demands consistency in its characters, because without it they are unrecognizable and the story is inchoate, the stage can more nearly approach the truth of protean human nature, because each character already has a local habitation and a name, in the actor and the actor's costume. Critics and audiences of our time, who come to theater after having learned to manage the conventions of the novel, fail to see the irrelevance of their demand for consistency of characterization and squirm at the sudden conversions in Shakespeare's plays. The playwright is perfectly aware of the gratuitousness of such conversions and of the tension between the happy ending he can impose by art and the improbability of such a solution in real life, but by such means he can show by analogy the action of grace.

No sudden change of personality has been more difficult for Shakespeare critics to allow than the change of the scapegrace Prince Hal into the hero of Shakespeare's historic epic, King Henry V. He announces it to his dying father and the audience in full awareness of its incredibility:

> If I do feign,
> O, let me in my present wildness die,
> And never live to show th'incredulous world
> The noble change that I have purposed!
>
> *(4.5.151–54)*

He calls his majesty "a new and gorgeous garment," which is how his altered status is first perceived by the audience, who must wait to see whether such vestments actually fit him. The office of king is continuous: "The king is dead, long live the king." Henry expresses the change that has taken place in himself as if he had become his father.

> And I do wish your honors may increase
> Till you do live to see a son of mine
> Offend you and obey you, as I did.
> So shall I live to speak my father's words . . .
>
> *(5.2.104–7)*

To make the point again even more strongly, he speaks in strange paradoxes:

> My father is gone wild into his grave,
> For in his tomb lie my affections;
> And with his spirits sadly I survive
> To mock the expectation of the world,
> To frustrate prophecies, and to raze out
> Rotten opinion, who hath writ me down
> After my seeming.

> *(5.2.123–29)*

The audience, "the world" in Henry's phrase, has no option but to judge him after his seeming, for "What may be digested in a play" is conveyed by feigned action and words learned by rote. In order to create a situation in which the audience may feel the utterness of the change in Henry's nature, Shakespeare deliberately builds the scene of confrontation with Falstaff into a truly shocking *coup de théâtre*. He allows us to entertain the notion along with Falstaff that the elevation of his "tender lambkin," his "sweet boy," to the throne will mean good times for all his old boon companions. The audience ought to feel as surprised and convinced by the change in Henry as Falstaff does.

> Presume not that I am the thing I was;
> For God doth know, so shall the world perceive,
> That I have turn'd away my former self;
> So will I those that kept me company.

When thou dost hear I am as I have been,

Approach me, and thou shalt be as thou wast . . .

(5.5.56–61)

The coronation of an English monarch was and is still a sacrament, involving a series of sacramental signs (visible actions which signify a spiritual change), of which the most important is the one shared with baptism, confirmation, ordination, and extreme unction, namely the anointing. Henry can no longer mock at the state because he has become the state. His own desires for personal gratification are all subjugated to his priestly office. It is pointless to object that Henry is here untrue to himself, when the point is that the old self has been destroyed. We are supposed to feel that the change is miraculous, however unwelcome such a feeling might be to our modern sensibilities. In fact, the change is no more gratuitous and remarkable than those that revivalist preachers claim to witness every day.

The idea that human souls can regenerate themselves at will is fundamentally optimistic. It is also profoundly anti-Calvinist. In Shakespeare's view, which was the view of most of the English Christians of his time, Protestant or Catholic, human potential was delimited by grace. No matter how potent the working of evil in tempting human frailty, divine intercession was always within the reach of prayer. No one's damnation was foreordained. The Christian "conspectus" or "theater" in the old sense has a happy ending, whether the protagonist triumphs or is damned, because God's justice has been done. Given the Christian schema, Elizabethan tragedy cannot supply inevitability. It is perhaps because scholars felt that lack of irrevocability enfeebled Shakespearean drama that they seized on a speech from *Hamlet* as offering a new, Elizabethan kind of inevitability. The destruction of the tragic hero could be seen as an ineluctable consequence of his own nature.

> So, oft it chances in particular men
> That for some vicious mole of nature in them,
> As in their birth, wherein they are not guilty
> (Since nature cannot choose his origin),
> By their o'ergrowth of some complexion,
> Oft breaking down the pales and forts of reason,
> Or by some habit, that too much o'erleavens
> The form of plausive manners—that these men,
> Carrying, I say, the stamp of one defect,
> Being Nature's livery or Fortune's star,
> His virtues else, be they as pure as grace,
> As infinite as man may undergo,
> Shall in the general censure take corruption
> From that particular fault. The dram of evil
> Doth all the noble substance often doubt
> To his own scandal.

(1.4.23–38)

The commonest explanation of the tragedy of *Hamlet* is by reference to the "fatal flaw" of indecisiveness, as it is to Macbeth's ambitiousness, or Othello's jealousy, all considered as fixed aspects of personality as inescapable as anatomy or race—yet in this passage Hamlet is principally referring to the effect of a conspicuous flaw on the way an individual is perceived by others, who are blind to his virtues and characterize him by his one failing. It is quite possible to watch a modern Hamlet bumbling and dithering around the stage, shadowboxing with his own personality, especially when the part is played in a cinematic inward-turning way, with much the same feelings as one might watch a disabled person trying to climb the Empire State Building, but to do so is to experience rather less than the play has to offer. The audience of Shakespearean tragedy does not have to sit paralyzed by pity and terror, awaiting the passive catharsis of these potentially noxious feelings. Rather, they are actively involved in understanding, interpreting, and judging, swinging between commiserating and condemning, identifying and rejecting.

In order to understand the necessary questions of the play (in Hamlet's phrase) the audience must be drawn into the feelings of the characters, which are displayed for them in monologues, but at the same time they are never allowed to forget their separate existence *qua* spectators. The action of Shakespearean drama is carefully distanced in time and space, topped and tailed with choric commentary. Shakespeare uses all the mechanisms of alienation—self-conscious reference to the theatrical situation, interpolated songs, synopses, dumb shows, mask figures, comic interludes, anachronisms, topical references, and schematic or symbolic representation of abstract ideas. The audience's own set of values is always relevant; the suspension of disbelief is never total. It is this aspect of Shakespeare's art which scholars have had the most difficulty in understanding and applying. It is of course an essential feature of his thought, which cannot be correctly conveyed without an attempt to show how the ideas emerge in play dialogue, which involves not only the dramatis personae but the feeling and thinking horde of spectators as well.

Perhaps the role for which the American actor Edwin Booth (1833–93) was most renowned was Hamlet. This 1873 lithograph depicts the actor in character as the Danish prince.

Hamlet, and Heroic Doubt

The most consistent demonstration of this dramatic dynamic at work is the play of *Hamlet*, which corresponds exactly to Sidney's definition of tragedy in the *Apologie*:

> High and excellent Tragedy, that openeth the greatest wounds, and showeth forth the ulcers that are covered with tissue; that maketh kings fear to be tyrants, and tyrants manifest their tyrannical humors; that with stirring the effects of admiration and commiseration, teacheth the uncertainty of this world, and upon how weak foundations gilden roofs are builded . . .

In his 1580 essay "An Apologie of Raymond Sebond," the French essayist Michel de Montaigne (1533–92), depicted in this portrait by Daniel Dumonstier, argued that every Christian has a right to use his God-given intelligence in striving to find the right way, but should not assume that reason can supplant faith and acceptance of the inscrutable will of God.

The play is a guided tour through a lying world, the foundations of which slip and slide, so that we doubt not only what we see and hear but our own powers of judgment and action. The mood is very much that of Montaigne's "An Apologie of Raymond Sebond," and there are verbal echoes of Florio's translation of the *Essais* in the play, but while the fellowship between the spirits of Shakespeare and Montaigne is indubitable, it is important also to remember that the paradoxicality of the human condition was apparent to all Elizabethan thinkers. As Sir John Davies confesses in *Nosce Teipsum*:

> I know my bodie's of so fraile a kind,
> As force without, feavers within can kill:
> I know the heavenly nature of my minde,
> But 'tis corrupted both in wit and will:
> I know my soule hath power to know all things,
> Yet she is blinde and ignorant in all;
> I know I am one of nature's little kings,

>   Yet to the least and vilest things am thrall.
> I know my life's a paine and but a span,
>   I know my Sense is mockt with every thing:
>   And to conclude, I know mysell a Man,
>   Which is a proud, and yet a wretched thing.

What Sir John Davies knows is actually that he knows nothing: irony is the natural mode of the Christian skeptic. This kind of thinking is the prelude to the development of tolerance and pluralism, but there is nothing flaccid about it. Doubting is a strenuous business; in the case of Hamlet it is heroic. His spiritual heroism is ironically contrasted throughout the play with the physical heroism of Fortinbras, who blindly carries through his own revenge action without questioning its morality. Hamlet may torment himself with his inability to redeem his family honor by mass slaughter, indeed must torment himself, but the way he has chosen, though painful and dangerous, is the right way.

>   . . . to my shame I see
> The imminent death of twenty thousand men
> That, for a fantasy and trick of fame,
> Go to their graves like beds, fight for a plot
> Whereon the numbers cannot try the cause,
> Which is not tomb enough or continent
> To hide the slain . . .

(4.4.59–65)

By the time they hear this soliloquy, audiences have traveled a long way through the slick and greasy world of Elsinore with Hamlet for their guide. The intimacy of his contact with them is established from his first appearance as a spectator at Claudius's elaborate performance as king in council, when before he speaks to any character on stage he speaks to the audience. In reply to his mother's questioning of his mourning behavior, he makes a claim which the audience has no choice but to believe:

> 'Tis not alone my inky cloak, good mother,
> Nor customary suits of solemn black,
> Nor windy suspiration of forc'd breath,
> No, nor the fruitful river in the eye,
> Nor the dejected havior of the visage,
> Together with all forms, moods, shapes of grief,
> That can denote me truly. These indeed seem,
> For they are actions that a man might play;
> But I have that within which passes show . . .

> *(1.2.77–85)*

Thus he places himself as it were between the audience and the histrionic behavior of Elsinore; the audience recognizes him and accepts him as belonging to a different order of reality. He will show them falsehood in its endless disguises, but in doing so, because the mind herself cannot be trusted, he will be in danger of corruption and derangement.

After his first soliloquy, when Hamlet emerges as protagonist, the audience acquires a new surrogate onstage, as Horatio comes to tell Hamlet what the audience already knows. The intimacy between audience and protagonist is strengthened by the protagonist's display of affection for this silent watcher, to whom as he lies dying Hamlet entrusts his hard-won truth:

> O God, Horatio, what a wounded name,
> Things standing thus unknown, shall I leave behind me.
> If thou didst ever hold me in thy heart,

Absent thee from felicity awhile,

And in this harsh world draw thy breath in pain

To tell my story.

(5.2.349–54)

In the third scene of *Hamlet*, we are shown Elsinore at home; we hear Laertes traducing Hamlet, and Polonius intoning his con-

This 1842 painting by the Irish artist Daniel Maclise depicts the moment in *Hamlet*, act 3, scene 2, in which Hamlet watches Claudius for any signs of guilt during the performance of a play in which a man kills a king and subsequently woos the widowed queen. The model for Maclise's Hamlet was his friend the Irish actor William McReady, who took the role in a touring production of 1823.

ventional advice to a son with the principal emphasis upon cunning and manipulation, followed by his attempt to instill the same politic calculation in his daughter. Normally the convention requires us to believe what is said on stage about an absent character unless it is specifically denied, but Ophelia's dimness ("I do not know, my lord, what I should think") and Polonius's brutal cynicism incline us to withhold belief. When Hamlet at his next appearance condemns the general tendency to believe the worst of people, our doubts are justified. The audience, through Horatio, its surrogate, swears loyalty to Hamlet, undertaking to keep faith with him, no matter how strangely he should behave. Again, a Hamlet scene is followed by a scene without him, in which we discover for ourselves what lies behind Polonius's glib, high-sounding morality. We see him paying a spy to defame his own son so vilely that the snooper himself protests. Ophelia, a spy herself, comes hotfoot to tell of Hamlet's first piece of odd behavior. Polonius interprets it as love madness; the audience has no reason to respect his judgment. It seems more likely that Hamlet was searching in Ophelia's face for something that he did not find, something which is not to be found in Elsinore.

The disjunction between how the inhabitants of Elsinore see Hamlet and the way the audience experiences him is deliberately maintained, for the audience must learn to disbelieve Elsinore on its own account. They will respond positively to the appeal in Hamlet's love letter to doubt "truth to be a liar" rather than doubt him. Gradually he is assuming the role of probe, searching the body of Elsinore for the source of its corruption. If we doubt his right to be "scourge and minister" to Denmark's disease, the play collapses into chaos, but if we forget the danger of sliding into solipsism, which is always present when we trust to our own reason for a guide, we have not understood the nature of the case. The drama of Protestantism in its finest hour was the heroism of insisting upon the sovereignty of the individual conscience.

Hamlet's first diagnostic tool is a play: the neatness of the correspondence of play within play to the play itself is a typical example of the kind of ingenuity that delighted learned Elizabethans. The action that Hamlet mounts is extremely formal, with its elaborate dumb-show, its prologue, and its long speeches in rhyming couplets. What is contained within this stylized structure is the "occulted truth" that is causing the disease of Denmark. All around Hamlet, Elsinore is presenting feigned actions of a more naturalistic variety, which convey nothing but lies. Ophelia pretends to read, to lure Hamlet into a play staged by Polonius for the hidden audience of Gertrude and Claudius. Gertrude summons him to her closet, to play a scene for Polonius. Each time the audience is privy to the setup, and each time Hamlet guesses right.

The Elizabethan audience knew the conventions of revenge tragedy at least as well as we today grasp the complicated rules of spy fiction. Once Hamlet has raised the suspicion that he knows that Claudius is a murderer, he is in deadly danger, not only of being eliminated by the tyrant, but also of being damned himself. The scourge of God is afterward burned in the fire. In case we should forget this conundrum, the scene where Hamlet decides not to kill Claudius as he is praying helps us to remember it. By failing to kill Claudius, Hamlet comes off the revenge treadmill, and instantly becomes the hunted rather than the hunter. When Rosencrantz and Guildenstern come yapping at his heels, he cries, "Hide, fox, and all after." The audience knows exactly what he means, but his stage hearers are nonplussed. Only Claudius himself, sharing the audience's knowledge, knows what Hamlet is up to. He evades confrontation, preferring to hide and spy as if he were the avenger and not Hamlet. We begin to see that if Hamlet is to redeem Denmark, he will have to die to do it. The *flagellum dei* is being replaced by the *Christus medicus*. Hamlet himself refers to his task as surgery: "I'll tent him to the quick" (2.2.593; cf. 3.2.296–97). Claudius borrows Hamlet's imagery in an ironic reversal; he sees Hamlet as the disease, and his poisons and Laertes's sword as the lancet and tinctures that must cure it (4.3.9–10, 69–70; 4.7.122). The greater action is moving inexorably to its close, but a new peril is at hand. Hamlet may fall victim to the general contagion and become as morally numb as his fellow Danes.

The actual disease of Denmark is not a giant conspiracy but rather a lack of curiosity and concern about matters unseen. The Elsinoreans are content to keep up appearances and muddle along, keeping in the good graces of the powerful. Their apathy has permitted the usurpation of the throne by a truly evil man. When Hamlet sets about to wring his mother's heart, he is trying to awaken her moral sense. His real opponent is not Claudius's criminality, but the spiritual blindness which allows him to exist. To dispel that blindness (and sharpen the moral sensibility of the audience) it is not sufficient to take a life for a life. The appearance of Osric, the mask of everyday evil, bearing the weapons that will carry out the fatal surgery, is the culmination of our exploration of falsehood.

A did comply with his dug before a sucked it. Thus has he—and many more of the same bevy that I know the drossy age dotes on—only got the tune of the time and, out of an habit of encounter,

a kind of yeasty collection, which carries them through and through
the most fanned and winnowed opinions; and do but blow them to
their trial, the bubbles are out.

(5.2.184–91)

Hamlet goes toward his death in a Christian spirit of resignation. He
forestalls Horatio's offer of a way out in words reminiscent of Matthew
10:29 and 24:44: "There is special providence in the fall of a sparrow. If
it be now, 'tis not to come; if it be not to come, it will be now; if it be not
now, yet it will come. The readiness is all" (5.2.215–18).

He asks pardon of his murderer, like a man settling scores before
death. For the first time the audience knows what he does not know and
cannot guess, that he is going like a lamb to the slaughter. Before he can
physic the evil of Claudius he is himself dying; only then does he force
Claudius to feel the potency of his own poisons. The surgery is complete.
In Horatio's arms, he takes his leave of the audience.

You that look pale and tremble at this chance,
That are but mutes or audience to this act,
Had I but time . . .
                    O, I could tell you—
But let it be. Horatio, I am dead,
Thou livest. Report me and my cause aright
To the unsatisfied.

(5.2.339–45)

The audience has come a long way from the beginning of a conventional revenge tragedy, the breadth of the chasm between Hamlet's

perception and Laertes's blind rage. The journey is impossible without the revenge convention which is the fixed point from which it takes off, and against which, personified in both Laertes and Fortinbras, it constantly measures itself. What the audience has experienced is not simply the spectacle of a skeptic, but the actual stress of doubting and confrontation. Elizabethans were used to disputation, preaching, and all forms of rhetorical polemic as we are not; even so, modern audiences, however unused to hearing extended speeches in the dense language of a Renaissance wit, are enthralled by *Hamlet*, as long as its metaphysical action is expounded to them by the actor.

Macbeth: Sin and the Action of Grace

Shakespeare's achievement as a thinker, then, is not that he formulated original notions or erected a new system of philosophy, but that he took the commonplaces of Elizabethan thought and made them actual. What he found was a hybrid and rather unsystematic cluster of useful ideas; what he did was give them concreteness and actuality, "a local habitation and a name." His overriding concern was, in modern theater parlance, "to take the audience with him." All other considerations, the unities of time and place and kind, whether "tragedy, comedy, history, pastoral, pastoral-comical, historical-pastoral, tragical-historical, tragical-comical-historical-pastoral, scene individable, or poem unlimited" (*Hamlet*, 2.2.392–96), were irrelevant.

Irrelevant too is the question of whether *Hamlet* is a true tragedy, seeing that Horatio (and the audience) are both reasonably sure that their hero will be sung to his rest by "flights of angels." Plays which ended in salvation were usually called comedies, but in Shakespeare's time the term also included plays like *All for Money, Common Conditions, The Tide*

Tarieth No Man, The Longer Thou Livest the More Fool Thou Art, Enough Is as Good as a Feast, Liberalitie and Prodigalitie, which end with the damnation of their protagonists. Their authors presented them, as in the prologue of Thomas Lupton's *All for Money* (1578),

> Beseeching God, the hearers, that thereby shall be touched,
> May rather amend their faults, then therewith be grieved.

These "very merry and pithy comedies" dealing with matters "pitiful and strange" are the forebears of *Macbeth*. The structure of *Macbeth* is very simple. The greatness of the protagonist is established; he is tempted, he falls, and is eventually destroyed. The temptation comes from without, not in this case as a Vice but in the form of the witches. It is

The British artist Henry Fuseli painted this image of Macbeth and the witches in 1783. Fuseli, born Johann Heinrich Füssli in Switzerland in 1741, translated *Macbeth* into German when he was a teenager. Fuseli was so imbued with Shakespeare that some called him Shakespeare's painter. From 1786 he was a main contributor of Shakespearean subjects to the Boydell Gallery; he exhibited paintings of Shakespeare subjects to the annual exhibitions at the Royal Academy, as well as designing thirty-seven illustrations for *The Plays of William Shakespeare*, edited by Alexander Chalmers (1805).

important in the play that the audience meet the witches before Macbeth does and know, as Macbeth does not, that they have the powers of fallen angels, subject to neither space nor time. They speak in Hudibrastics, the meter of burlesque, only to be expected of the lineal descendants of the imps of Satan on the popular stage.

The commission of mortal sin requires grave matter, full knowledge, and full consent. In Macbeth, Shakespeare creates a character who (unlike Faustus, for example) is capable of all three, of carrying out the act, of knowing exactly how heinous his crime is, and of sticking to it once done. The irony is of the bitterest: Macbeth is damnable because he is a hero. Yet his damnation is not inevitable. Because he is more spiritually aware than anyone else on the stage, Macbeth himself reminds us of the existence of heaven and the action of grace. The tempters know their limitations: only God has power over life and death and only the individual can bring about his own damnation. As they say of the tormented pilot (and by extension Macbeth), "Though his bark cannot be lost, / Yet it shall be tempest-tost" (1.3.24–25).

Macbeth's vulnerability to the witches is not caused by excessive superstition on his part, but by corrupt desire which moves him to take a false step: he misinterprets the fact that two of their predictions have come true. His self-delusion is willful. As Duncan's chief champion, Macbeth's career so far has been ruled by loyalty: as soon as he conceives the notion of ruling for himself, he is already corrupted. The scourge of Duncan's enemies cannot contemplate kingship for himself without imagining turning his sword against the king. Although he faintly tells himself: "If Chance will have me King, why, Chance may crown me, / Without my stir" (1.3.144–45), he already feels guilty. If it were not for his awareness of guilt, the next tempter, his wife, would have little to work on.

In January of 1889, the British actress Lillie Langtry (1853–1929), who became a U.S. citizen in 1897, traveled to New York to make her debut as Lady Macbeth. According to Charles Harlen Shattuck, author of *Shakespeare on the American Stage*, "What Mrs. Langtry offered was not the traditional virago . . . but a womanly, wifely, loving Lady Macbeth, certain of purpose . . . seducing Macbeth rather than driving him." This photograph of Langtry as Lady Macbeth was taken by Benjamin J. Falk.

Lady Macbeth sneers at her husband's tenderness of conscience (1.5.16–21), but ironically it proves her best ally, for she argues that as he has already desired the crown in his heart and envisaged the murder of the king, the only obstacle to his carrying out the act is fear, itself dishonorable. Again, Macbeth allows himself to be misled by false reasoning. The audience, like heaven, "the judicious sharp spectator," watches as Lady Macbeth makes her horrific appeal to the powers of evil:

> Come, you Spirits
> That tend on mortal thoughts, unsex me here,
> And fill me, from the crown to the toe, top-full
> Of direst cruelty! make thick my blood,
> Stop up th' access and passage to remorse;
> That no compunctious visitings of Nature
> Shake my fell purpose, nor keep peace between
> Th' effect and it! Come to my woman's breasts,
> And take my milk for gall, you murth'ring ministers,
> Wherever in your sightless substances
> You wait on Nature's mischief! Come, thick Night,
> And pall thee in the dunnest smoke of Hell,
> That my keen knife see not the wound it makes,
> Nor Heaven peep through the blanket of the dark,
> To cry, "Hold, hold!"

(1.5.40–54)

As befits the utterance of evil, the speech is riddled with inconsistencies. One cannot ask a power which waits upon nature's mischief to overrule nature, just as one cannot hide any act from the eye of heaven, here referred to as an audience. The actual audience, like the heavenly one, can peep through the blanket of stage dark, and what it sees is that a compunctious visiting of nature prevents Lady Macbeth from carrying out the act at all. Grace abounds to the chief of sinners: Macbeth is vividly aware of the forces opposing his terrible act. Duncan's virtues

> Will plead like angels, trumpet-tongu'd, against
> The deep damnation of his taking-off;
> And Pity, like a naked, new-born babe,
> Striding the blast, or heaven's Cherubins, hors'd
> Upon the sightless couriers of the air,
> Shall blow the horrid deed in every eye,
> That tears shall drown the wind.

(1.7.19–25)

He could, like Banquo, ask the Powers, one of the ranks of angels, to protect him from cursed thoughts, but instead, futilely, he too asks that his act remain unobserved:

> Thou sure and firm-set earth,
> Hear not my steps, which way they walk, for fear
> Thy very stones prate of my where-about.

(2.1.56–58)

The earth he speaks of is the wooden promontory of the stage, watched by hundreds of eyes, some of whose owners must have felt like crying, "Hold, hold!" Repentance is always close at hand, but Macbeth rejects it. The consequence of his terrible deed is that now, even when he tells the truth, he has to be lying.

> Had I but died an hour before this chance,
> I had liv'd a blessed time; for, from this instant,
> There's nothing serious in mortality;
> All is but toys: renown, and grace, is dead;
> The wine of life is drawn, and the mere lees
> Is left this vault to brag of.

> *(2.3.91–96)*

This is Macbeth's feigned lament for the death of Duncan: he says it hypocritically, but every word of it is true. Critics have had difficulty with the sudden appearance of crass burlesque in the play, in the form of the Porter and his grotesque parody of the sophistical arguments about desire and performance, and the pantomime degeneration of the witches' scenes, but if we consider that Macbeth's life has become tragic farce, we can see both as correlatives of absurdity. Macbeth is trying to kill his soul, which as resolutely refuses to die. Guilt joins forces with grace to prompt him to repent but he will not. He is too paralyzed by despair to consort with his wife or exert himself to rule the kingdom he has won. He is learning that the powers of evil are not to be relied upon and waits to see if the powers of good will assert themselves. Lady Macbeth, deluded about the nature of the powers of darkness and her own, dies raving. In his dark and meaningless world Macbeth makes a half-hearted attempt to force the witches' prophecies to his will, and, failing, curses them—

Infected be the air whereon they ride;
And damn'd all those that trust them!

(4.1.138–39)

thus wishing his own damnation.

So far there has been no hint in the play that any antidote to Macbeth's evil is at hand. The first sound of an innocent human voice since the murder is stifled when Macbeth's hirelings kill Macduff's little boy. In the next scene, Malcolm quizzes Macduff about his failure to protect his family, as if he, like the audience, had begun to doubt whether any man worthy to vanquish Macbeth could be found. Macduff cries out,

Bleed, bleed, poor country!
Great tyranny, lay thou thy basis sure,
For goodness dare not check thee!

(4.3.31–33)

Then, in one of the most improbable exchanges in the Shakespeare canon, Malcolm, after having said,

Angels are bright still, though the brightest fell:
Though all things foul would wear the brows of grace,
Yet Grace must still look so.

(4.3.22–24)

traduces himself with boundless lechery, "staunchless avarice," and total depravity, at which last Macduff jibs, unable to serve a man who would

Pour the sweet milk of concord into Hell,

Uproar the universal peace, confound

All unity on earth.

(4.3.98–100)

Having been thus reminded of the virtues needed in a king, as Malcolm enumerates them, "Justice, Verity, Temperance, Stableness, / Bounty, Perseverance, Mercy, Lowliness, / Devotion, Patience, Courage, Fortitude," we are prevented from spending too much time wondering why Malcolm misrepresented himself by the introduction of the theme of the saintliness of Edward the Confessor, and his hereditary gift for curing scrofula.

With this strange virtue,

He hath a heavenly gift of prophecy;

And sundry blessings hang about his throne,

That speak him full of grace.

(4.3.156–59)

The theme of redemption and grace, the mode of its operation, having been stated, it is immediately grasped by Macduff who sees that his sins have been expiated not by him but by his wife and children.

Did Heaven look on,

And would not take their part? Sinful Macduff!

They were all struck for thee.

(4.3.223–25)

Macduff's submission to divine will and repentance of sin enable him to proceed against Macbeth: "The Powers above / Put on their instruments" (4.3.238–39). Their instruments are Malcolm and Macduff.

At Dunsinane, solipsism still prevails. In her deranged dream, Lady Macbeth is still telling herself that what's done is done and there is no power which can punish sin. "What need we fear who knows it, when none can call our power to accompt?" (5.1.35–37). What maddens Macbeth is the thought that she may be right, life may never have made more sense than it now does to him, unable to feel terror or pity: "Direness, familiar to my slaughterous thoughts, / Cannot once start me" (5.5.14–15). His wife's death cannot bring a tear to his eye, being merely one more nonsense in the tale "Told by an idiot, full of sound and fury, Signifying nothing" (5.5.27–28).

The monstrous joke played on him by the witches has not yet reached the punch line, but already Macbeth has begun to laugh. He knows that he is the butt, like a baited bear (5.7.1–2), even while he imagines that, in telling him that no man of woman born would kill him, the witches meant that no earthly man could overcome him. When Macduff tells him that the joke is on him,

> Despair thy charm;
> And let the Angel, whom thou still hast serv'd,
> Tell thee, Macduff was from his mother's womb
> Untimely ripp'd,

(5.8.13–16)

Macbeth finally realizes that the forces of evil do not serve men.

Macbeth lives as an exemplum of the perverted hero, because of Shakespeare's ability to give life to every stage of his disastrous career.

The aspects of his character which are developed successively, and draw him on, are suggested in the dense and allusive blank verse with such vividness that we are tempted to erect whole theories of his personality structure upon them, but *Macbeth* resists this process much better than *Hamlet*. The character insists upon its universality, just as the stage persists in being a kind of no man's land, an isthmus in a sea of cosmic forces, a world where we may all be lost, except "by grace of Grace."

Modern audiences are usually aware of *Othello*, *Hamlet*, and *Macbeth* as great character studies offering opportunities for great performances. The three roles are most often given to actors of great range and technical virtuosity so that the average playgoer is more aware of their utter unlikeness to himself than of what he has in common with them. If we restore the didactic dimension to Shakespeare's dramaturgy and consider the demands made upon the audience's belief and disbelief, we can see even these heroic figures as exemplars of the human struggle for salvation. Like his contemporaries, Shakespeare was fascinated by human variability, and could create all kinds of human grotesques out of quiddities of speech and mannerism, yet such creations, however elaborate, are never ends in themselves but exist as ornaments or intensifications of the central concerns in the plays. Modern sensibility tends to see complex characters like Othello or Macbeth or Hamlet as case histories, and modern criticism cannot get much out of the yearly revivals of such plays without entering into elaborate psychoanalyses of their heroes. But the theater is fundamentally different from the schoolroom and the newspaper column. What happens there is still immediate and innocent; what shakes the heart is not a judicious calculation of the precise kind of personality flaw which affects the hero, but the gradual revelation of the sublimity of the moral universe in which he moves. Because we share the hero's language we can struggle through its chasms and steeps with him.

Shakespeare does not provide us with a map of an ethical system. It would be futile to attempt to extrapolate from his works any collection of ethical imperatives, if for no other reason than that he shared with his contemporaries a profound and vivid sense of morality as something organic and dynamic, which was not given to any individual to understand in its entirety. The playwright's task was not to expound it, but to convey a lively and unforgettable impression of its reality.

Again, it is an unassuming remark of Wittgenstein's which shows a way into Shakespeare's conceptual world:

> Shakespeare displays the dance of human passions, one might say. Hence he has to be objective; otherwise he would not so much display the dance of human passions, as talk about it. But he displays it to us in a dance, not naturalistically.

By following this insight through its implications, we may begin to see how essential is Shakespeare's invisibility and how irrelevant his opinions.

FOUR

Politics

●

The History Plays: Shakespeare's Epic Theater

It seems likely that Shakespeare made his reputation initially by his history plays.

> How would it have joyed brave Talbot (the terror of the French) to think after he had lain two hundred years in his tomb, he should triumph again on the stage, and have his bones new embalmed with the tears of ten thousand spectators at least (at several times) who, in the tragedian that represents his person, imagine they behold him fresh bleeding!

At the beginning of Act 5, scene 3, of *Henry VI Part I*, Joan la Pucelle—Joan of Arc—invokes a group of spirits (here depicted as fiends) and asks for their aid in France's fight against England. When the spirits desert her, she realizes her cause is lost. The scene is depicted in this 1803 engraving, by James Lee, of a work by British artist Henry Fuseli (1741–1825).

Thomas Nashe is probably referring here to *Henry VI Part I*, while Greene's envious reference to Shakespeare dates from the same period and quotes another play from the trilogy, evidently in the full expectation that it will be familiar to his readers. The magnitude of Shakespeare's success can be guessed not only from the bitterness of Greene's resentment, but by comparing Nashe's figure with the total population of London in 1592.

In our time such success has only been achieved by cinema blockbusters, and it is perhaps to them rather than to our own "legitimate" theater that we should compare Shakespeare's vast chronicle. Just as the movie moguls turned their screens over to patriotic propaganda during the Second World War, the playwrights of London, dependent upon court protection against the wrath of the Puritan city corporation, vied with each other to produce plays which would function as epic histories for the illiterate, forcing the unsynthesized manifold of historical fact and surmise into the instant but momentary logic of the drama, described by the Prologue to Shakespeare's antihistory, *Troilus and Cressida* (26–29):

> . . . our play
> Leaps o'er the vaunt and firstlings of those broils,
> Beginning in the middle, starting thence away
> To what may be digested in a play.

In *Henry V* each act is prefaced by a Chorus which exhorts the audience to cooperate with playwright and actors by vigorous exercise of imagination.

> . . . pardon, gentles all,
> The flat unraised spirits that hath dar'd

On this unworthy scaffold to bring forth
So great an object: can this cockpit hold
The vasty fields of France? or may we cram
Within this wooden O the very casques
That did affright the air at Agincourt?
O, pardon! since a crooked figure may
Attest in little place a million,
And let us, ciphers to this great accompt,
On your imaginary forces work.

(Prologue, 8–18)

The lists of instructions pepper the Choruses with imperative verbs: "suppose . . . play with your fancies . . . behold . . . hear . . . do but think . . . Follow, follow! Grapple your minds to the sternage of this navy . . . leave . . . Work, work your thoughts. . . . Still be kind, / And eke out our performance with your mind" (3, Chorus, 34–35).

The unsteadiness of the tone, with its odd combination of didactic superiority and deprecation of the talents of playwright and players, could indicate the nearest thing we have to a self-defense mounted by Shakespeare, or at any rate a defense of the epic theater. *Henry V* is the last play to be written in a spectacularly successful series. It is the centerpiece of the sequence; all the plays look forward and back to the emergence of the quintessential British hero, King Harry. For most of Shakespeare's adult life, England had been struggling to resist Spanish expansionism, fueled by the plunder of the New World. The queen's interest in the booty that could be seized from Spanish galleons was not simply greed but necessity. A series of continental wars had so depleted the English exchequer that she was forced to resort to various kinds of unpopular emergency taxation, while the common people lived in continual fear of impressment for active service. Shakespeare's portrait of Falstaff as a corrupt recruiting officer has always been appreciated as comic; its implications go far deeper. Falstaff confesses that he has "misused the king's press damnably" and "got in exchange of a hundred and fifty soldiers three hundred and odd pounds." Those of his hearers

who would "rather hear a devil than a drum" doubtless laughed hard at this, but their laughter cannot have sounded so carefree when Falstaff (in *Henry IV Part I*) described the sequel: "I have led my ragamuffins where they are peppered; there's not three of my hundred and fifty left alive, and they are for the town's end to beg during life" (5.3.36–38).

Because he is entertaining, scholars persist in finding excuses for Falstaff, forgetting perhaps that the Vice was always an ingratiating, lively, and amusing fellow. Falstaff's ancestor is the

Elements of Shakespeare's Falstaff can be found in the character Good Fellowship, one of several stock characters in medieval morality plays. Other characters—including Virtue, Vice, Free Will, and Contemplation—appear on this page from a 1510 edition of *Hickscorner*, a morality play written some time between 1497 and 1512.

Morality figure of Good Fellowship, who always lets people down and cannot bring the protagonist one step on his way to heaven. Perhaps by showing a familiar kind of parasite who preyed upon the common people in this risible fashion, Shakespeare was offering the resentment of voiceless people some vent. Corruption of those in public office was certainly widespread in England in the 1590s; it seems possible that Falstaff excited not only laughter but jeering and catcalls.

The overriding concern of the historical dramatist was not, however, to give focus to public resentments, but to create an epic theater, using all the resources of verse, music, and pageantry to project a vivid impression of the continuity of history and the audience's place in it. As Shakespeare's fellow historian Samuel Daniel pointed out in his answer to Thomas Campion's attack on rhyme, the historical poet's concern was at least partly mnemonic: "All verse is but a frame of words confinde within certaine measure; differing from the ordinarie speache, and introduced, the better to expresse mens conceiptes, both for delight and memorie." The fame of the patriotic speeches in Shakespeare's histories is the best evidence that he succeeded in creating the incantations with which people stay their hearts in times of trouble. The histories of the staging of Shakespeare could be supplemented by the story of the use of Shakespeare in wartime. In the darkest days of the siege of Malta (1941–43), to stir the hearts of the war-weary, groups of servicemen used to get up amateur radio performances of *Henry V.* Nowadays the art of "psyching" people up for a superhuman effort has been elaborated into something rather sinister. By comparison Shakespeare's way of awakening dormant heroism in his audience is both modest and subtle.

For those people who believe that propaganda cannot be art, or that propaganda in support of causes of which they disapprove, such as loyalty to the monarchy, to a religious sect, or willingness to die for one's country, cannot be good art, the history plays will raise serious difficulties, which are only partly resolved if we decide to treat them as self-contained poetic entities or psychological studies of individual kings and nobles. For one thing, we will have to ignore a good deal of commentary presented by nameless characters, by representative characters, and by lay figures who appear for one important speech and are never seen again. For another, we will have difficulty with ghosts and portents, prophecies and curses, and we will have to ignore anachronistic contemporary references. *King John*, for example, contains various elements which have less to do with history than with propagandist intention—anti-papal (3.1), anti-Spanish (2.1.23, 26; 3.3.2; 5.1.65; 5.2.151, 154; 5.7.117), and pro-Elizabethan, in the parallels between John and Elizabeth—yet it is by no means crass or oversimplified. The complexity of the issues is never minimized, but

thrown into dramatic relief by the selection of incidents and manipulation of sympathy. While we are drawn into the psychology and dynamic of conflict, at the same time dogmatism and faction are shown to be inappropriate responses, always involving more error than justification.

By the time he wrote *Henry V* (1598–99) Shakespeare must have been aware that the illusion of unity in English society could no longer be sustained. It was no longer in the power of the dramatist to hold the imagination of all, literate and illiterate, powerful and powerless. The development of the indoor theaters with their greater scenic resources and their prurient interest in matters sensational and intimate rather than public-spirited and universal had divided the Globe's audience while other entertainments vied for the groundlings' half-pence. The most talented newcomers to write for the theater had a different viewpoint at once loftier and more limited.

In 1598 a play of Ben Jonson's had been accepted for performance by the Lord Chamberlain's Men at the Curtain. Jonson had been

Dutch mapmaker Claes Janszoon Visscher's 1616 panorama of London shows, in the foreground, the Bear Garden Theatre (directly under the word "Thamesis") and the Globe Theatre (to its right). Both were partially open to the air.

imprisoned in 1597 for his part in the seditious play *The Isle of Dogs*, the playing of which resulted in the closing of all the London theaters from July to October. Less than a year later he was tried at the Old Bailey for killing one of Henslowe's players in a duel. He was convicted and escaped hanging only by pleading benefit of clergy. He was branded on the thumb and all his possessions confiscated by the Crown. He was practically unemployable in the theater, but with the playing of *Every Man in His Humor* by Shakespeare's company his fortunes were reversed. It is therefore hardly to his credit that when he revised *Every Man in His Humor* he added a censorious prologue which could be thought to apply specifically to Shakespeare:

> Though need make many poets, and some such
> As art and nature have not better'd much;
> Yet ours for want hath not so loved the stage,
> As he dare serve the ill customs of the age,
> Or purchase your delight at such a rate,
> As, for it, he himself must justly hate:
> To make a child now swaddled to proceed
> Man, and then shoot up, in one beard and weed,
> Past threescore years; or, with three rusty swords,
> And help of some few foot and half-foot words,
> Fight over York and Lancaster's long jars,
> And in the tyring-house bring wounds to scars.

Jonson dismisses the whole epic theater, together with the chorus that "wafts you o'er the seas," the deus ex machina descending from the clouds, depictions of hell-fiends surrounded by fireworks, and, significantly enough, tempests made by shaking shot in a sieve or playing drumrolls. Jonson is concerned with "realism" or "truth to life," but Shakespeare deliberately eschewed this more insidious kind of illusion, knowing that the truest poetry was the most feigning. The apology he makes in *Henry V* is an inverted boast of his power to transport audiences to a vantage point from which they could oversee and interpret their own history, and of their willingness to be so transported.

> And so our scene must to the battle fly;
> Where, O for pity! we shall much disgrace
> With four or five most vile and ragged foils,
> Right ill-dispos'd in brawl ridiculous,
> The name of Agincourt. Yet sit and see;
> Minding true things by what their mock'ries be.

(4, Chorus, 48–53)

The historical dramatist had worse to fear than the sneers of the literati. No play would be licensed if it was thought to meddle in matters of politics or religion. When *The Book of Sir Thomas More* was submitted to the Master of the Revels, he stipulated that the scene of the insurrection of the Lombards be deleted from the play. The deposition scene was removed from *Richard II* both on stage and in the printed quartos by about 1597, and the 1600 quarto of *Henry IV Part II* contained extensive revisions. A comparison of the 1594 quarto of *Henry VI Part II* with the version in the First Folio shows that all possible references to the Irish question, Elizabeth's legitimacy, rebellion, or to particular noble families had at some stage been deleted from the text.

The licensing authorities could sniff out political and religious allegory in the most unlikely places. The old queen loved theater; indeed

Queen Elizabeth I (1533–1603) reigned over England and Ireland for nearly forty-five years, from 1558 until her death. The elaborate portrait of the monarch seen here, known as the Armada portrait, was painted by Elizabeth's Sergeant Painter, George Gower, and is currently on display at Woburn Abbey in Bedfordshire, England. It depicts the defeat of the Armada and the driving of the Spanish fleet onto the rocks. The queen's right hand rests on a globe; her finger points to the Americas.

she was herself a hieratic figure in an allegorical pageant of queenship which became more elaborate as she grew feebler. As she strained royal privilege to raise money for the war with Spain and parliamentary pressure for reform began to intensify, the common people were racked by a concatenation of visitations of plague, poor harvests, a wave of new enclosures, and economic recession. Fear of popular rebellion culminated in the law of 1595 prohibiting assemblies. The historical playwright had a clear brief; if he was not prepared to put together chronicles which would unite his audiences in their duty to God and the Crown, he had better stick to some other medium. In order to avoid the pitfalls of historical playwriting, it was not enough to refrain from trampling the queen's corns. The playwright had to approach the struggle to subdue the tangle of confusing anecdote knowing what lesson he wanted it to teach and prepared to discard, distort, and invent in order to present his own version of the meaning of history.

Shakespeare's principal sources for the histories are Raphael Holinshed's *Chronicles of England, Scotland, and Ireland* (1577, 1587) and Edward Hall's *The union of the two noble and illustre fameles of Lancastre and York* (1548). Neither is followed to the letter. Shakespeare suppresses matters irrelevant to his dramatic purpose, inverts the order of events, creates important roles for individuals of no historical importance, and telescopes lifetimes into single scenes. Critics and scholars once presumed that Shakespeare had simply amplified Holinshed's *Chronicle* in a more or less unsystematic fashion. Gradually more painstaking sifting of Tudor historiography showed that he had consulted virtually all of the available sources, including some which existed only in manuscript, some never translated from the French or Latin, and some which had never been written down at all but survived by oral transmission. His method was not to evaluate all in order to select one and follow it consistently, but to pick and choose from mutually conflicting accounts the versions of individual events which best suited the dramatic depiction of his vast theme, the making of the Tudor monarchy out of the chaos of the Wars of the Roses.

When Shakespeare digests and transmutes material gathered from both written and verbal sources, the resulting compound is subject not only to the imprint of his personality but the exigencies of theatrical exposition. We find in a Shakespearean history as we find in Brecht's *Galileo* that the climactic episodes have been set in a framework of commentary. Where Brecht uses song or projected words upon a screen, Shakespeare is more likely to use choric characters who may utter highly wrought poetic speeches of some length only to disappear for the rest of the play. In *Henry V* he elaborates the commentary into a Chorus which is more than ever Brechtian in that it constantly refers to the historic reality beyond the diminished shadow which is all that the play can present. For Brecht the characters themselves are less important than the historical dialectic that they represent; the same is true of Shakespeare, but the concept of history is very different. His historical theater must first of all create an epic dimension, using every resource, not only drums, trumpets, banners, heraldry, and high-sounding words, but the imagination of the audience. The protagonist is England, manifest not only in the noble individuals who represent the body politic, the anointed kings, but in the audience itself. The point is made in many different ways, that king and people interdepend, that each individual is a microcosm of the state, that states like the souls of men must be redeemed.

In an age when religious zeal turned brother against brother, the drama sought to reunite the people and raise public morale. Shakespeare was remarkably successful in managing potentially inflammable material so as to send audiences home excited and gratified rather than anxious about the deteriorating political situation and increasing instability of the Elizabethan order, but the plays are neither insipid or jingoistic. Shakespeare demonstrates his own version of the truism that those who fail to learn the lessons of history are compelled to repeat them; by signs, portents, and prophecies, events to come are foreshadowed while past causes are also tied in to present action, in each of the eight plays covering the two hundred years between the revolt of the Percys and the accession of Henry VII. None is easy watching: not only must audiences follow attentively the fortunes of war expressed in emblematic skirmishes of a handful of soldiers with banners, drums and trumpets, and wooden swords, they must trace the endless permutations of subtle themes, constantly resurfacing in altered forms. The weaving together of the huge themes of right and wrong rule, of kingship as a divine

Richard the 3ᵈ King of Englãd and France, Lord of Ireland

Richard III (1452–85, né Richard Plantagenet), the last monarch from the House of York, ruled England from 1483 until his death at the Battle of Bosworth Field. This likeness of Richard—note that he is not depicted as a hunchback—was etched by Wenceslas Hollar (1607–77).

office and a Machiavellian political institution, of the reciprocal duties of ruler and ruled, against such a vast panorama is only possible in the theater and then only in poetic drama.

Shakespeare's achievement is the more remarkable because he began his series in the middle, with the *Henry VI* plays, in about 1590. The next episode of the sequence to be written was chronologically the last, *Richard III*, announcing the coming of the Tudors and the dawn of England's golden age. *Richard III* may be a libel on a dead monarch, but it is also an extraordinary amalgam of poetic and theatrical resources, resulting in a figure far more impressive and interesting and no less complex than its historical original. Richard himself has clearer bloodlines in literature than in history: he is Vice, Machiavel, Senecan tyrant, and Marlovian hero, and at the same time kin to Mercutio and Hamlet, the plainspoken critics of hypocrisy and affectation. The England of *Richard III* is as rotten as Denmark: the moral scheme of the play involves the punishment of turpitude by a devil in human form, as might regularly be seen on any English stage. The difference is that Richard is so various, so brilliant in his invention, and so appallingly alive in Shakespeare's version, that the audience must realize with a shock that it is attracted to unblushing evil.

The Office of Kingship: *Richard II*

Shakespeare's play of *Richard II* exists alongside another play on the same theme, *Woodstock*, by an unknown rival. There were also anonymous plays of King John and Richard III, while in 1595 Samuel Daniel produced his historic epic, *Of the Civile Warres betweene the two Houses of Lancaster and Yorke*. All the evidence points to a self-conscious desire to create a national literature. Shakespeare's *Richard II* is close in spirit to Daniel's work and may actually be indebted to it, among a number of other possible influences. Yet despite the variety of its sources, the play in no way smells of the lamp. To see just how strenuously its audience must cooperate in following the drama of inevitable usurpation and the invocation of its fearful aftermath, there is no better course than to examine more closely the weaving itself.

In the first scene, Richard is the king in word and deed, presented as the arbiter in a quarrel between two of his nobles. In the next scene, John of Gaunt, whose character is developed quite independently of historical precedent, reveals that the instrument of the death of the Duke of York, of which Bolingbroke has accused Mowbray, was in fact Richard himself.

> God's is the quarrel—for God's substitute,
> His deputy anointed in His sight,
> Hath caus'd his death; the which if wrongfully,
> Let heaven revenge, for I may never lift
> An angry arm against His minister.
>
> *(1.2.37–41)*

It is a mistake to interpret the fact of Richard's anointedness as signifying a belief in absolute monarchy. He is a figure of Christ, but subject himself to the law of God and morality. If he has countenanced murder in order to safeguard the security of his throne, he is deeply compromised, but Gaunt is simply orthodox in saying that the king's crime does not warrant his own crime against the king. The duel is a way of leaving the arbitration to God, and it is therefore the more startling when Richard calls it off in the next scene, although we see at once that, if the king himself is guilty, he cannot let matters take their course. It is the worse, then, when he palters with the terms of banishment, allowing Bolingbroke to return in six years, Mowbray never. The theme of the passionate love of the Lancasters for England sounds in the lament by Bolingbroke for the country he must leave. In scene 4 Richard tells us that this love is reciprocated by the people, and reveals that he regards his kingdom as his to exploit for any purpose of his own, commons and nobles alike.

Act 2 opens with Gaunt on his deathbed denouncing Richard's attachment to his own pleasures, while his brother, the Duke of York, describes him as attentive only to "praises . . . lascivious meters" and reports "of fashion in proud Italy." Richard's attachment to things non-English is set against Gaunt's patriotic fervor, expressed in his "other Eden" speech, which ends with the roundest condemnation of Richard's attitude:

> This land of dear souls, this dear dear land,
> Dear for her reputation through the world,
> Is now leas'd out—I die pronouncing it—
> Like to a tenement or pelting farm . . .
> That England, that was wont to conquer others,
> Hath made a shameful conquest of itself.

> (2.1.57–60, 65–66)

The king was the head of the body politic; he and the state were one substance like man and wife. In plundering England to finance the indulgence of his expensive foreign tastes, Richard is preying on himself. Taking his privilege as a dying man and the king's uncle, Gaunt remonstrates with him, calling him England's landlord rather than her king. Richard tells him that if he were not the son of his grandfather, he would be executed for such treasonable talk. Gaunt's last words accuse him of the murder of his other uncle, the Duke of Gloucester. Richard sequesters his goods in defiance of York's pleas for the rightful claim of Bolingbroke, and leaves for Ireland. The choric trio of Northumberland, Willoughby, and Ross summarize the sufferings of England under Richard's rule before Northumberland announces the return of Bolingbroke leading a rebellion against the Crown, with the success described to the queen by various witnesses in the following scene. As Richard has won himself no allies in the pillaged realm, trusting too far to his right of succession, he is soon left with nothing else. By contrast, Bolingbroke is loved by all who serve him. "Base men by his endowments are made great," says Willoughby (2.3.138), thus broaching the great Renaissance debate on the relative merits of nobility by birth and nobility of character. No sooner is the theme broached than we glimpse the ironic possibility that loss of kingship may ennoble Richard while gaining it destroys Bolingbroke's integrity. Bolingbroke gives his solemn oath that he has come not to usurp the throne but simply to reclaim his rightful goods and title. The act ends with a choric scene announcing the demoralization and defeat of the loyalist troops.

In act 3, after the scene of summary justice meted to Richard's favorites, we find him caressing English soil as he returns from his Irish campaign. He luxuriates in his sacerdotal role, unwilling as ever to hear good advice. He applies to himself the Platonic image of the sun, which by its mere appearance dispels the reign of night.

> Not all the water in the rough rude sea
> Can wash the balm off from an anointed king;
> The breath of worldly men cannot depose
> The deputy elected by the Lord.

(3.2.54–57)

The Wilton Diptych was painted by an unknown artist in the late 1390s. In the left foreground, King Richard II (1367–1400) kneels before the Virgin Mary and the Christ child. Edmund the Martyr, Edward the Confessor, and John the Baptist stand behind Richard. Eleven angels flank Mary, one of whom holds a flag bearing the Cross of St. George, the emblem of England.

The news brought by Salisbury and Scroope finally brings home to him the fact that, though the balm of kings cannot be removed, they can drown. It is difficult, given the tradition of post-Ibsen drama, not to make of Richard's highly charged and mutually inconsistent speeches at this point an aspect of his personality. It is more "profitable," in terms of Renaissance theory, to consider what they display of the central ideas in the play. Richard boasts that God will send angels to defend his deputy, and finds that he has nothing but angels. The answer to his question, "Is not the king's name twenty thousand names?" (3.2.85) is "No." He curses Bushy, Bagot, and Greene in words very similar to Matthew 23:33, and likens himself to Christ betrayed by Judas, only to discover that his old cronies died loyal to him. In the magnificent exordium, "Let's talk of graves, of worms and epitaphs" (3.2.145ff.), he draws a surreal picture of the vulnerability of kings:

> . . . within the hollow crown
> That rounds the mortal temples of a king
> Keeps Death his court, and there the antic sits,
> Scoffing his state and grinning at his pomp,
> Allowing him a breath, a little scene,
> To monarchize, be fear'd, and kill with looks . . .

(3.2.160–65)

Having learned his lesson, too late, Richard would exert himself to defend his crown, but learns that with the defection of York there is no hope. So the play arrives at the crux, the meeting of the king by right with the king by acclaim. Bolingbroke is still loyal; Shakespeare takes pains to depict him as an unwilling usurper because the political conundrum is the point; though readers for centuries after might tease themselves about whether Bolingbroke is hypocritical in his challenge (3.3.31–67), that question is the result of reading and pondering, not of response to the dramatic situation. It is the more ironic that Bolingbroke and Richard should both foretell a tempest of blood in England's green land. For a brief space it seems that the two can agree, but Richard sees that in repealing Bolingbroke's banishment, and restoring his lands, he has capitulated to a greater power and reduced the monarchy to a nonsense: "What must the king do now? Must he submit?" (3.3.143). Bitterly he reiterates the word "must," knowing that he must, as Bolingbroke's hostage, accompany him to London.

As we might expect after a climactic scene of this kind, what follows is a scene of choric commentary. The queen, as she has done before, plays the part of a chorus foretelling woe, preparing the way for the Duke of York's gardeners, who in lofty blank verse describe Richard's basic error, which is not to have exploited the riches of England for his own ends, for that lies within royal privilege, but to have allowed a serious rival to grow up to threaten his throne. Shakespeare could have found his parallel of the state with a garden in any of dozens of sources, but the central idea here is pure Machiavelli: the sovereign's first duty to the Crown is to make sure he keeps it. The gardener answers the queen's questions about the fate of her husband with an image which is basic to the structure of the play:

> Their fortunes both are weigh'd;
> In your lord's scale is nothing but himself,
> And some few vanities that make him light.
> But in the balance of great Bolingbroke,

Besides himself, are all the English peers,

And with that odds he weighs King Richard down.

(3.4.84–89)

Act 4 begins with the scene that was censored in the last years of Elizabeth's reign. She had complained to the antiquary Lambarde that a tragedy of Richard II had been "played 40tie times in open streets and houses." She may have been referring to earlier performances of Shakespeare's play, blaming herself that they had been countenanced. The queen's famous remark, "I am Richard, know ye not that?" could have been parried by pointing out that she was also Henry IV, the office of king being continuous, but in the months following Essex's abortive rebellion she was unlikely to take the point. On the eve of the rebellion, some of Essex's supporters had approached Shakespeare's company, asking them to revive *Richard II* in a special performance. When the players objected that the play was old and they would lose money, the performance was subsidized by the not inconsiderable amount of 40 shillings.

The Bishop of Carlisle forces the deposition scene, on the grounds that no subject has the right to judge "the figure of God's majesty, / His captain, steward, deputy elect," only to be arrested by Percy, the only character in the play who has consciously harbored treason in his heart. Richard has already abdicated in favor of his cousin, but is forced to enact the scene, which he too describes in terms of tipping scales (4.1.184–89). He conducts his own deposition from center stage, reducing Bolingbroke, whose heroic stature has dominated the play so far, to a Pilate figure. The scales are moving again: as Bolingbroke falls in the audience's estimation, Richard will rise with the acting out of his passion and death. The first agony is the farewell to his wife, and here Richard shows that he has understood the relationship that should have prevailed between him and England:

> Doubly divorc'd! Bad men, you violate
> A two-fold marriage—'twixt my crown and me,
> And then betwixt me and my married wife.

(5.1.71–73)

While rebellion festers and Henry IV embarks upon the long struggle which is the subject of the whole epic sequence, Richard awaits his death, an inevitable concomitant of Henry of Lancaster's need to consolidate his power. He dies heroically, while the erstwhile hero of the play is reduced to equivocation and cowardice by the demands of policy. The stage is set for the plays of Henry IV which followed two years later. We have learned of young Henry's wild ways, we have seen the unscrupulousness of the elder Percy, and we have heard the reiterated prophecy of civil war and the desolation of England.

"Negative Capability"

There is nothing innovative in Shakespeare's idea of history, no ideology or philosophy which he imposed on the material that he organized. Rather he took the mass of mutually conflicting notions which he found expressed in the Bible as interpreted by his contemporaries, the homilies, the chronicles, broadsides and ballads, popular plays and traditions, and in the compendia of wisdom from all kinds of sources, and made of it something remarkably exciting and alive, repaying all kinds of analysis and suggestive of all kinds of alternatives. Keats called Shakespeare's

The English poet John Keats (1795–1821) defined negative capability as a state in which "man is capable of being in uncertainties, mysteries, doubts without any irritable reaching after fact and reason." This portrait of Keats was painted by Joseph Severn, a friend of the poet.

faculty for allowing mutually conflicting notions full imaginative development "negative capability."

The inclusiveness of Shakespeare's intelligence is a characteristic that he shared with many of his contemporaries. The compilers of collections of *sententiae* and proverbs did not concern themselves with whether the wisdom they culled from the ancients was consistent or could supply some feasible rule of life. It was unimportant that if one aphorism was true another on the same page would have to be false. Schoolboys learned to think and to write by applying generalizations to particular cases, and to develop the dry *sententiae* so that they became alive and interesting they produced examples of the ways in which these propositions became true or were realized. They were not asked to erect philosophical systems on the basis of selected premises, but to consider the kind of truth inherent in all of them. Nowadays students of logical form might call this kind of compendious thinking "fuzzy logic." The term does not imply a value judgment: what it really refers to is the protean nature of all concepts, and the importance of the ambiguous area which lies around the nucleus of definition, as the white lies around the yolk of the egg. *Definitio est negatio*; in Shakespeare's mind concepts were alive, growing, changing, proliferating, and dying, like man himself. Nowadays, logicians, shocked into humility by the capacity of mathematics to confound their notions of certainty, are beginning to recognize what they are pleased to call "paraconsistency." By a similar process, secular Renaissance philosophers like Pierre de la Ramée and even Bacon and Montaigne sought to open the mind to all kinds of protean possibility rather than to mechanize its operations in the development of a system. A modern parallel could be sought in the Wittgenstein of the *Investigations*.

For those of us who are not students of logical form, Shakespeare's myriad-mindedness has a more obvious kind of value. The era that was "undistinguished" in logic was unparalleled in its fruitfulness: out of its rich confusion were born all the modern sciences. In creating the kind of organic unity which could keep disparate elements in his own version of the Heraclitean dance, Shakespeare displays the mentality that made possible the development of the pluralism and tolerance that came, after a period of agony, to characterize English political thought and institutions. Freedom from aggressive certainty makes possible the emergence of consensus, the art of compromise. Like Montaigne, Shakespeare saw that human reason was essentially fallible and understood the mechanism of rationalization long before it had a name. Some commentators have sought an encapsulated statement of his political position, and found it in the speech of Ulysses in *Troilus and Cressida*.

> Degree being vizarded,
> Th'unworthiest shows as fairly in the mask.
> The heavens themselves, the planets, and this center
> Observe degree, priority, and place . . .

> *(1.3.83–86)*

Not one Shakespearean audience but would feel cheated by the thought that all the debating in his plays adds up to nothing but this, a schoolboy's essay on the topos "When degree is shak'd . . . the enterprise is sick." As we have seen in a too-brief discussion of the dynamics of the first play of Shakespeare's history sequence, Shakespeare's frame of reference was Heraclitean not static; the dancers are not only moving in the dance, but the dance is moving and changing too.

Dancing (bright Lady) then began to bee,
When the first seeds whereof the World did spring,
The fire, ayre, earth and water—did agree,
By Love's perswasion,—Nature's mighty King,—
To leave their first disordred combating,

    And in a daunce such measure to observe,

    As all the world their motion should preserve.
Since when, they are still carried in a round,
And changing, come one in another's place:
Yet do they neither mingle nor confound,
But every one doth keepe the bounded space
Wherein the Daunce doth bid it turne or trace:

    This wondrous myracle did Love devise,

    For dauncing is Love's proper exercise.

FIVE

Teleology

•

The Vision of Entropy: *King Lear*

After he had completed his history sequence by adding *Henry V*, Shakespeare abandoned English history, until some time between 1603 and 1606 when he wrote *King Lear*. The story was known from at least one old play, from Holinshed, from *The Mirror for Magistrates*, and from *The Faerie Queene*. This time, Shakespeare did not carefully mix and match in order to supply a coherent dramatic demonstration of historical and political issues. He did not build character upon factual indications left by the chroniclers, but catapulted the action into a region beyond human history, denying man's right to impose his own interpretation of the meaning of life or to demand satisfaction in the way that events are ordered.

This photograph shows the American actor Edwin Forrest (1806–72) in the role of King Lear, which he performed in 1872 at the Globe Theatre in Boston—his last role.

There is a strange reluctance in scholars to admit that *King Lear* is about senility, perhaps because they feel that to admit that Lear's brain is aging is to diminish his heroic stature. The point of course is exactly that: however great the hero, to this he must come, if he has the misfortune to live so long. The play has two strands: one is the strand of optimism, the belief that there is a providence in the fall of a great man as in the fall of a sparrow; the other, the strand of rage against the dying of the light. Shakespeare cannot have known the second law of thermodynamics, but he did know that on earth we have no abiding city.

> Nativity, once in the main of light,
> Crawls to maturity, wherewith being crown'd,
> Crooked eclipses 'gainst his glory fight,
> And Time that gave doth now his gift confound.
> Time doth transfix the flourish set on youth,
> And delves the parallels in beauty's brow,
> Feeds on the rarities of nature's truth,
> And nothing stands but for his scythe to mow.

(Sonnet LX)

"Time's thievish progress to eternity" is a principal theme of the sonnets, which take the *carpe diem* theme beyond the conventional lament for the passing of youth and beauty. Shakespeare does not reject "the wide world and all her fading sweets" in order to contemplate the joys of heaven in the *de contemptu mundi* tradition, but keeps his eye fixed on the created universe, arriving at something more like a vision of entropy. In the Lear world, more is lost than can be replaced. The king is a figure of man, the crown of creation, with "knowledge and reason" "the marks of sovereignty." As the king loses his temporal power, so humanity must lose these marks of sovereignty, if indeed they were ever truly evident, for man may be deluded about his importance in the scheme of things.

Shakespeare's view, at least in *King Lear*, seems close to Montaigne's and has some useful points in common with the post-Darwinian view. The audience, like Tennyson, becomes more aware of the need for a "larger hope," the more faintly it feels that it can trust to it. The possibility that there is anything divine in the human version of God's likeness recedes.

The first scene of *King Lear* has caused a good deal of caviling. It is hieratic, unmotivated, preposterous. Most of the protesting has come from critics who prefer to think of Shakespeare as a naturalistic playwright; some has come from those who consider that if Lear causes his own suffering he is not a tragic figure. The point after all is the same as that made in Montaigne's "Apology for Raymond Sebond": we are not masters of our souls, for our capacity to master ourselves is subject to myriad distortions. Lear is confused, paranoid, arbitrary; he behaves in the manner typical of sufferers from atherosclerosis of the brain, grown old without ever being wise. In relinquishing his power he bows to necessity, but his notion that by dividing the realm he may still control it is a Machiavellian delusion. Such delusion is a common case: many old people forced into dependency upon their children and their children's spouses burn emotional energy in futile machinations for power and are cast out on to our own versions of the heath as a result. The descent from the sixth to the seventh age of man, from "lean and slippered pantaloon" to "second childishness and mere oblivion, / Sans teeth, sans eyes, sans taste, sans everything" (*As You Like It*, 2.7.165–66), is long and dreadful.

In most of his plays, as in *Hamlet*, Shakespeare takes the usual theatrical view of old men, "that their faces are wrinkled, their eyes purging

Despite the tender solicitation Cordelia shows toward her father, King Lear, she refuses his demand for a declaration of love. This photograph of John Gielgud as Lear and Peggy Ashcroft as Cordelia—in act 4, scene 7, when Lear is asleep in a chair and Cordelia kisses him—was taken in 1950 for a production at Stratford-upon-Avon.

thick amber and plum-tree gum, and that they have a plentiful lack of wit, together with most weak hams" (2.2.197–200). Comedy is forever young and sees the palsied old from without; tragedy does not normally deal with anything so mundane or inescapable as the decay of the mind. The attitude of Goneril and Regan to their father is vile and comprehensible at the same time. Cordelia, in reminding her father of the limitations of her duty toward him, is simultaneously just and cruel. Hamlet may rage at being constantly humored; Lear insists on it and unjustly punishes those who refuse. He casts out his daughter in unfatherly fashion and then laments the ingratitude of his daughters. Kent remonstrates with him, calling him *mad*, and *old man*, accusing him of *folly* only to be banished for his pains. Irrational rages afflict the sclerotic; Lear goes far beyond what is reasonable in his cursing of Cordelia. Goneril and Regan know as well as the audience what causes Lear's craziness: " 'Tis the infirmity of his age . . .", "the unruly waywardness that infirm and choleric years bring with them."

Up to the beginning of act 3, Lear has made little appeal to our sympathy. Instead he returns scorn for scorn, invoking curses, commanding the elements to enact his personal vengeance. The disowned daughter, so "unnaturally" treated by her capricious father, has enlisted our sympathies by confiding the truth of her love for him to the audience. The Fool rides his master, continually holding up to him the fact of his own folly, while Lear misses point after point:

LEAR: Dost thou call me fool, boy?
FOOL: All thy other titles thou hast given away; that thou wast born with.

(1.4.154–56)

This sally of the Fool's places *King Lear* in the august tradition of the *Praise of Folly*. Erasmus's fool in God is as a child, for unless we become as little children we cannot enter heaven. It ill behooves man to boast before God of his intellectual achievements and the temporal wealth and power he has managed to secure, for all was done by grace of God and is as nothing compared to the wisdom and power of God. The typical fool in God is nimble-witted, light-hearted, unassuming, and stoical. In knowing his own foolishness the fool is disabused, and therefore saner than another man, like Lear, who refuses to take account of his own foolishness and help-lessness. A fool is a "natural," *simple* as we say, and by extension, still in a state of nature. We are all born in this condition, and if we live so long we will die in second infancy. The born idiot avoided all the temptation and sin associated with the development of intellectual faculties, so he was thought of as perpetually innocent, or marked by God, "touched." Our word *silly* is descended from an Old English word meaning "blessed," surviving still in our idea of blissful idiots. The survival of these connotations into present-day English indicates something of the frame of reference within which Shakespeare's wise fools moved, a frame of reference which is profoundly skeptical and profoundly Christian.

Edmund too is a natural, in this case a natural son, a bastard. The contrast between the bastard's self-image and the Fool's is part of the intricate play on mutually contradictory notions of what constitutes nature. Every character in *King Lear* bandies the word "nature" and in no two cases does it mean quite the same thing. Edmund strides to the front of the stage, talking not to the audience but to nature, addressing her as his goddess. Commentators have said that Elizabethan audiences would have been shocked at such idolatry; Edmund evidently thinks that he is singled out for her service by virtue of his bastardy, which he imagines gives him greater vigor. As a Warwickshire landowner with large gardens at his charge, Shakespeare probably knew something of the greater vigor of hybrids: Perdita, in *The Winter's Tale*, rejects hybrid carnations—"We may call them nature's bastards." Edmund's view of nature is evidently something more like the process of natural selection, which we are told favors rape and bastardy. The Fool, besides being a natural, is also a natural philosopher, who supplies a selection of examples of animal behavior in nature. As no one on stage is listening, no one understands his examples of elimination of the unfit.

Amid the constant chime of the word "nature," a paradoxical pattern begins to emerge. While human beings use the word to indicate a loose bundle of properties of which they are in favor, and characterize the abhorrent as "unnatural," they in fact invoke a power which is profoundly indifferent to them. Lear is the first in the play to personify nature, when he calls Cordelia "a wretch whom Nature is asham'd / Almost t'acknowledge hers," taking it upon himself to read Nature's mind as it were, in an act of unwitting hubris. Those who see Edmund's idolatry of nature as shocking do not see that Lear shares it.

> Hear, Nature, hear! dear Goddess, hear!
> Suspend thy purpose, if thou didst intend
> To make this creature fruitful!

(1.4.284–86)

Lear dares to order his goddess as if she were a demon summoned up to do his bidding, his familiar. He does not notice the inherent contradiction in his command to her to send Goneril a "disnatur'd torment" in the form of a thankless child. Gloucester's Nature is neuter, but he is hardly less confident that it exists for the benefit of man: "These late eclipses in the sun and moon portend no good to us: though the wisdom of Nature can reason it thus and thus, yet Nature finds itself scourg'd by the sequent effects" (1.2.100–103). His view is ridiculed not only by Edmund, who holds nothing sacred, but also by Edgar. Both are aware that the realm of nature extends beyond the reach of anthropocentricity and that nature is profoundly indifferent to the fate of any single species, let alone any individual.

Lear throws himself upon his goddess's mercy, and finds none, yet he persists in ordering the elements to do what they would do whether he ordered them or not. He is still deluding himself that he is the lord of creation, unaware that, like the year itself, he has lived through his cycle of generation, his spring, his summer, his fall of leaf, and now his bitter winter. His striving "in his little world of man to out-storm / The to-and-fro-conflicting wind and rain" (3.1.10–11) is absurd.

When Shakespearean personages abandon their homes and take refuge in the wilderness, they come not to the manicured lawns of pastoral but to the harsh countryside of Elizabethan England, where famine had been known in more than one area in the closing years of Elizabeth's reign. Whether it be a wood outside Athens (a profoundly English wood for all that) or Windsor Great Park or the Forest of Arden, the "desert" or wilderness is always a testing ground in Shakespeare's plays. In *As You Like It*, Duke Senior, driven from his dukedom by a younger brother, felt "the icy fang / And churlish chiding of the winter's wind" and congratulated himself with the thought:

> This is no flattery. These are counselors
> That feelingly persuade me what I am.

(2.1.10–11)

What the Duke refers to is clearly not his rank and breeding but his essential human nature. Once Lear ceases to think of himself as lord over creation and begins to consider himself part of it, he too may discover what his own nature is.

In the central act of the play, we see Lear's apotheosis. Stripped of everything, even faith in his clutch of mixed deities, he finds his kindred in a gang of ragamuffins. In case the achievement of fooldom be seen to be too easy, we are given another fool, a professional religious maniac who imposes his bizarre visions on credulous country folk. Edgar disguises himself as one of the Bedlam beggars

> who, with roaring voices,
> Strike in their numb'd and mortified bare arms
> Pins, wooden pricks, nails, sprigs of rosemary;
> And with this horrible object, from low farms,
> Poor pelting villages, sheep-cotes, and mills,
> Sometime with lunatic bans, sometime with prayers,
> Enforce their charity.

(2.3.14–20)

Tom o'Bedlam is the opposite of the Erasmian fool, for his religion is fabricated of grotesque superstitions, cemented by paranoid delusions of diabolical persecution, which have been turned to profit by imposing upon genuinely simple people. The religious maniac's solecisms are erected into an antirational system, the ultimate expression of man's mad pride.

The Christian skeptic might doubt the adequacy of reason in scrutinizing the ways of God, but he did not jettison it for a morass of compounded self-delusion. Tom o'Bedlam confesses his sinful past life to Lear and the Fool, calling himself "hog in sloth, fox in stealthiness, wolf in greediness, dog in madness, lion in prey," but Lear does not heed his inverted boast, believing what he sees rather than what he hears. "Is man no more than this? . . . Thou ow'st the worm no silk, the beast no hide, the sheep no wool, the cat no perfume . . . thou art the thing itself; unaccommodated man is no more but such a poor, bare, forked animal as thou art" (3.4.105–11).

Lear is beginning to see man as a species among species and to realize that if human life has value it cannot reside in state or in the "marks of sovereignty, knowledge, and reason" but in the lowest common denominator of humanity, even such as he in whom "Nature . . . stands on the very verge of her confine," the weak, the poor, the imbecile. Earlier in the play, he had upbraided Regan for denying him his retinue as unnecessary:

Allow not nature more than nature needs,
Man's life is cheap as beast's.

(2.4.268–69)

In his furious railing he had cursed the entire race of man, vainly summoning the impersonal powers of the elements to do his bidding.

And thou, all-shaking thunder,
Strike flat the thick rotundity o' th' world!

Crack Nature's moulds, all germens spill at once
That makes ingrateful man!

(3.2.6–9)

    The idea of germens or seeds, *rationes seminales*, derives ultimately from Saint Augustine, who held that the created universe contained material elements corresponding to the exemplars in the mind of God when he created and continues to create all that is. Nowadays we are more likely to think of them as genes or the genetic inheritance. As a poor, infirm, weak, and "despis'd old man," whose progeny have taken over the field of his

Act 3, scene 2, of King Lear begins with Lear and the Fool walking through a furious rainstorm. The scene is depicted here in an illustration by Albert Edward Jackson (1873–1952) from an edition of *Tales of Shakespeare*, a collection of stories based on the playwright's works by Charles and Mary Lamb.

erstwhile sovereignty, Lear is irrelevant to the process of "great creating nature." As Yeats wrote in "Sailing to Byzantium,"

> An aged man is but a paltry thing,
> A tattered coat upon a stick, unless
> Soul clap its hands and sing, and louder sing
> For every tatter in its mortal dress.

In act 3 of *King Lear* we witness the emergence and gradual ascendance of Lear's soul, in a series of scenes structurally akin to the low comedy written for the great clowns. The nearest parallels on the modern stage are the patter scenes between stand-up comics, which are the progenitors of Beckett's *Waiting for Godot*. The action moves into a region outside time as the Fool makes his ironic prophecy, which is actually a description by contraries of the status quo.

> [When] cut-purses come not to throngs . . .
> Then shall the realm of Albion
> Come to great confusion . . .

(3.2.88, 91–92)

Parasitism and hypocrisy, the Fool is saying, are part of the natural order. In a sentence, he destroys the illusion that the action is distanced within its pagan context, and dumps it into the audience's now: "This prophecy Merlin shall make; for I live before his time" (3.2.95).

The most extraordinary aspect of the achievement of this extraordinary play is the manner in which Shakespeare draws out Lear's soul, even as his mind decays. He begins to suffer from confusion, which he bears with great patience and the most moving anxiety. He gradually leaves off playing the ruler of the elements and begins to treat the people around him with humble courtesy, feeling for the first time the continuity of humanity.

> Take physic, Pomp;
> Expose thyself to feel what wretches feel,
> That thou mayst shake the superflux to them,
> And show the Heavens more just.

(3.4.33–36)

Lear's fleeting idea of social justice is kin to old Gonzalo's vision of the Golden Age in *The Tempest*. The old king like the old counselor is becoming a fool in God, as intellectual pride is purged by suffering. The interlude of peace as all the naked refugees foregather in an ineffectual attempt to understand their destiny is all too brief. We are twitched back to "civilization" to witness the blinding of Gloucester. The play's ironies turn unbearably bitter: Edgar reassures himself that there is a natural ebb and flow in human fortunes, "the worst returns to laughter," only to discover that human beings are capable of limitless pain: as Gerard Manley Hopkins was to say, "No worst, there is none." In Edgar's words, as he gazes upon his blinded father,

> . . . worse I may be yet; the worst is not
> So long as we can say "This is the worst."

(4.1.27–28)

Gloucester in his blindness sees more than he saw before, and his vision is much like Lear's. He gives his purse to poor Tom: "Distribution should undo excess, / And each man have enough" (4.1.70–71). The idea is not less moving because it is clearly beyond the human nature described by the Fool, in which Gloucester and Lear were happy to partake when they were in possession of their full powers of mind and body and privilege. However, as any sociobiologist knows, nature is not constructed solely of egotism. The survival of a species depends also upon altruism exercised within the group, generally by parents in favor of their young, but also by individuals in favor of the group. Albany recoils from the savage ethos in which his wife lives, foreseeing both her own destruction and that of the universe itself as a consequence of unbridled self-interest.

> Humanity must perforce prey on itself,
> Like monsters of the deep.

> _(4.2.48–49)_

If we put this insight into modern terms, we have the truism, "The successful species has no enemy but itself," having eliminated or controlled all others. In this sociobiological parable, it is fitting that the sisters destroy each other in competition for reproductive opportunity.

The most mysterious episode in _King Lear_ is the mock suicide of Gloucester. Edgar, a collection of masks rather than a character, chooses a new and shifting one for this charade in a sort of parody of salvation, and perhaps the last word on the human tendency to create gods in their own likeness who will behave in ways that humans can understand. If the play were a comedy, or at least a tragicomedy,

Edgar's victory over Edmund would have turned the tribulation to joy. As it is, their combat is both perfunctorily treated and irrelevant. Battered and bamboozled, Gloucester dies the joyous death of the faithful. Edgar has been unable to lengthen his life, but his lie, like Plato's magnificent myth, has made possible a good end. This is the counterpoint to the statements of the entropy theme. As Gloucester cries on hearing Lear's ramblings:

> O ruin'd piece of Nature! This great world
> Shall so wear out to naught.

(4.4.136–37)

Lear remembers that we come crying on earth, "that great stage of fools," and Edgar completes the thought:

> Men must endure
> Their going hence, even as their coming hither:
> Ripeness is all.

(5.2.9–11)

As Touchstone tells Jaques in the Forest of Arden, "from hour to hour we ripe and ripe / And then from hour to hour we rot and rot." Though this is not the whole story, it is an ineluctable part of the story. Art may devise palliatives for the waste of life, but they are no more true remedies than Edgar's lie or his quelling of Edmund. *King Lear* ends with a series of futile gestures. Albany restores Lear to his crown, but Lear makes no sign that he is aware of the fact, being too distressed by the death of Cordelia, the innocent truth-teller, whom he seems to confuse with the Fool, who has now disappeared from the play. As the king has gradually come to realize that he is "the fool of Fortune" he no longer needs the coxcomb shaken before him.

There is no way of reversing the "great decay," nor will Albany see the enactment of justice or vindication. The play ends with a deceptively pat couplet, which is Shakespeare's oblique statement of the law of entropy:

> The oldest hath borne most: we that are young
> Shall never see so much, nor live so long.

> *(5.3.325–26)*

It would be a mistake to interpret the futility of Lear's appeals to his gods as evidence of atheism on Shakespeare's part. Rather, like Montaigne, he denies man's right to scan the ways of God or to assume that God's will coincides at any point with his own. This Christian skepticism is neither pessimistic nor cynical, for it is based in acceptance of the benighted human condition. Its corollary is the rejection of all theories of *Übermenschlichkeit* or human perfectibility and with them any system of government which exalts the collectivity at the expense of the individual. If we press these related ideas further, we arrive at something more radical, a contempt for authoritarianism of any kind and a deep conviction of the equality of all human beings. Rank and power, like wit and beauty, are but lent, and interest must be paid:

> nature never lends
> The smallest scruple of her excellence
> But, like a thrifty goddess, she determines

Herself the glory of a creditor,
Both thanks and use.

(Measure for Measure, 1.1.36–40)

Kings are heroes in Shakespeare when they do not rely upon their state but humble themselves to the needs of their people, like Henry V walking among his troops on the eve of Agincourt. Richard II becomes a heroic figure when he recognizes his vulnerability and weeps not for himself but the country he failed to serve. The other kings in the chronicles never become heroes at all. King Lear becomes heroic when he is reduced to naked tramphood, tottering about the bare stage talking at cross-purposes like Vladimir to Estragon. In him two themes coalesce, the theme of sovereignty at the level of the state and at the level of the individual, and the theme of the dignity of the common man, though he be master of nothing, not even himself. Lear stands at the head of a line of nobodies, simply struggling to survive, whom Shakespeare allows to comment upon the actions of their betters.

"Naturals" and the Myth of the Golden Age

The justification for so long a discussion of *King Lear* in such a tiny book is that in that play Shakespeare shows us a stripped-down version of his mental landscape, free of decorative accretions, narrative encumbrances, and the formal demands of symmetry. Throughout his career he makes use of dreamlike structures, but nowhere do they stand so unadorned and inexcusable as in *King Lear*. An audience has no difficulty in following and feeling the tragedy, but because an essential element in it is the recognition and acceptance of humanity unadorned by beauty, health, or intelligence, scholars tend to find it perverse. In fact *King Lear*

The two Dromios (Dromio of Syracuse and Dromio of Ephesus) in *The Comedy of Errors* share some of the characteristics of Shakespeare's "naturals," who often serve as moral commentators. This ca. 1885 theater poster advertises a New York production of the play by the popular American acting duo of Stuart Robson and William H. Crane.

is the apotheosis of a theme which runs right through the Shakespearean canon, but is never given its full importance, because lowlife characters are considered (in the study, not in the theater and especially not in the Elizabethan theater) to be of secondary importance.

From the beginning of his career Shakespeare made use of lowlife characters as moral commentators. The action of *The Two Gentlemen of Verona*, in which a paragon of noble friendship tries to rape his friend's mistress, and the friend tries to make a present of her to him, is ironically distanced by the unwitting commentary of Launce and his adoring dog. The dog cannot be given away because he always comes back, while Launce for his part has "sat in the stocks for puddings he hath stolen."

The main action is elaborately Italianate, the commentary inveterately English. The Dromios in *The Comedy of Errors* have some of the same characteristics, but the next great natural must be "sweet bully Bottom" in *A Midsummer Night's Dream*. All these characters are garrulous, eager to explain and incapable of dissembling, unaware or unconcerned about the impression they are making.

In *Love's Labor's Lost* the yardsticks by which the affectations of lords, fantastical Spaniards, and pedants are measured are the clown, Costard, and the witty child, Moth. Costard's name signifies a kind of apple, and, by extension, derisively a head or "poll," which is the sense taken by Berowne when he calls him a "member of the commonwealth." He is caught up in the highfalutin games of his betters and mocks their pretensions to chastity and intellectual fervor by his unassuming spontaneity, while Moth deflates the arrogance of Don Armado and confounds the lords' amorous intriguings, prompted by nothing but his "father's wit" and "mother's tongue." When the lords' courtship founders on the rock of reality, the peasant and the child take over the stage and together with the schoolmaster and the curate successfully perform the old folk interlude of the debate of Hiems and Ver in its stead.

Christopher Sly, the drunken tinker who is woken by the lord's retinue in the Induction to *The Taming of the Shrew*, is another of these common denominators of humanity. If the pranksters who tell him that he is a lord expect him to make a fool of himself, they must be rather disappointed with the outcome, for Sly (unlike Malvolio, for example) resists delusion and remains himself in spite of their best efforts to beguile him.

The first professional fool in the canon is Touchstone in *As You Like It*, who is different from the country clowns in that he has no compassion.

He is a city clown, quick- if shallow-witted and eager to exploit the country people, dazzling them with fake sophistication. His name is not irrelevant, but his gibing wit, rather than proving the world of Arden false, proves it genuine. He skirmishes around the old shepherd, Corin, who has rather more to say about the facts of sheep-handling than suits with the pastoral convention, in Shakespeare's version of the perennial debate between court and country. Corin's simple statements stand at the kernel of the play: "Sir, I am a true laborer: I earn that I eat, get that I wear; owe no man hate, envy no man's happiness; glad of other men's good, content with my harm; and the greatest of my pride is to see my ewes graze and my lambs suck" (3.2.71–75).

As You Like It is the precursor of *King Lear* in a number of respects; the Forest of Arden is a harsh place and people who dwell there must make shift to survive. Like the heath, the forest is an anarchist community run on the principle of cooperation between equals. The Duke notes with pleasure that he has been leveled. The myth behind this depiction is one dear to English hearts, of England as she was before foreign invasion brought kingship and barony in place of the ancient system of wapentakes and hundreds. The notion of "Merrie England" is the English version of the myth of the Golden Age, and the essential concomitant of Shakespeare's belief that "now Nature bankrupt is, Beggar'd of blood to rush through lively veins." Later, the idea of a return to a way of life essentially British was to be intrinsic to the thinking of the Levellers and Diggers, who used the fantasy as Shakespeare shows Jack Cade using it in *Henry VI Part II*. " 'Twas never merry world since gentlemen came up," says one of the rebels, only to fall in behind a leader who is deluded that he is himself of noble blood. Cade's fantasy that when he is king "there shall be no money" is typical of anarchist Utopianism. Although

Shakespeare presents this crusade of the illiterate against the literate in a ridiculous light, he allows the rebels to make some telling points: "Thou hast appointed justices of peace, to call poor men before them about matters they were not able to answer. Moreover, thou hast put them in prison; and because they could not read, thou hast hang'd them" (4.7.39–43). When we meet Costard in *Love's Labor's Lost* he is being called about a matter he is not able to answer; the fact that educated people could escape hanging simply by reading a Latin verse must have struck some observers as a monstrous distortion of the law of *noblesse oblige.*

Nostalgia for a Merrie England that probably never existed is chauvinistic, but nostalgia for some Arcadia is a permanent aspect of European literature. It is not so much a time after all, as an idea of something enduring in human nature that is overlaid and distorted by surface changes. In the sonnets, Shakespeare represents himself as one of the old school, unskilled in persuasion and flattery, prompted only by the honest feelings of his heart. Plainspoken and tongue-tied sincerity was a rhetorical convention like any other, but Shakespeare clung to it, embodied in fool-poets, in chuckleheaded peasants and witty children. His blackest plays are those in which this value is unrepresented and humankind is without its anchor in simple goodness. The goddess Nature is an amoral pagan personification, her laws harsh and ineluctable. Disabused human nature, on the other hand, is our best resource, our best corrective for the cruelty and inequity of the human condition.

Shakespeare and Popular Wisdom

In popular literature, the debate between court and country was always won by the country, which was seen as the home of true love and loyalty, genuineness and generosity, industry and cooperation. Throughout his career, Shakespeare displays a deep attachment to native tradition, rather in the manner of Sir Philip Sidney, who wrote in his *Apologie for Poetry*: "Certainly, I must confess my own barbarousness, I never heard the old song of Percy and Douglas that I found not my heart moved more than with a trumpet; and yet it is sung but by some blind crowder, with no rougher voice than rude style." Even as sophisticated an observer as Orsino in *Twelfth Night* shares Sidney's susceptibility to the old songs, and seeks to impart it to Viola:

> That old and antic song we heard last night;
> Methought it did relieve my passion much,
> More than light airs and recollected terms
> Of these most brisk and giddy-paced times
> Mark it, Cesario, it is old and plain;
> The spinsters and the knitters in the sun,
> And the free maids that weave their thread with bones
> Do use to chant it: it is silly sooth,
> And dallies with the innocence of love,
> Like the old age.

(2.4.3–6, 43–48)

Throughout his career, Shakespeare used his own versions of simple song forms as a gentle corrective to the affectations of the wiser sort, who were often "folly-fallen." In *Twelfth Night*, the professional fool has the last word, in a song of "silly sooth," "When that I was but a little tiny boy." Feste's counterpart in *Lear* sings a verse of the same song, which divides the life of man into four categories, along the lines of the description of the role played by folly in childhood, youth, manhood, and old

The Bride's Good-morrow.

A folem feaft your comely cooks do ready make
    where all your friends will be feen.
Youngmen and maids do ready ftand,
With fweet rofemary in their hand,
    a perfect token of your virgin's life:
To wait upon you they intend
Unto the Church to make an end,
    And God make thee a joyfull wedded wife!

FINIS.

The Bride's Good-morrow.

To a pleafant new Tune.

[This is a peculiar, but a pleafing ballad, tinged with a puritanical fpirit, and unqueftionably of an early date, though, as we learn at the end of it, " Printed by the Affignes of Thomas Symcocke," of whom we have before fpoken (p. 26). The domeftic ceremonials, preceding a marriage, near the end of the reign of Elizabeth, are delicately touched, and afford a not uninterefting illuftration of the manners of the time. The lines near the clofe,

    " With fweet rofemary in their hand,
        a perfect token of your virgin's life,"

fhew why that herb was of old employed as an emblem at weddings, and afford a particular explanation of a paffage in " Pericles." Act iv. Sc. 6. The exclamation " Good morrow, Miftris Bride !" is found, as a quotation, in more than one play of the time of Shakefpeare, with other allufions to this ballad.]

THE night is paffed, and joyfull day appeareth
    moft cleare on every fide,
    With pleafant mufick we therefore falute you:
    good morrow, Miftris Bride!
From fleepe and flumber now wake you out of hand,
    your Bridegroome ftayeth at home,
Whofe fancy, favour and affection ftill doth ftand
    fixed on thee alone.
Dreffe you in your beft array;
This muft be your wedding day.

The popular music of Shakespeare's time was often disseminated as broadside ballads—i.e., ballads printed on big sheets of paper and hawked in the street. The ballads were dittied to popular tunes that had accompanied older ballads, such as "The Bride's Good-morrow," which Shakespeare certainly knew (see pages 177–78). The lyrics were reprinted in the compilation entitled *A Book of Roxburghe Ballads*, published in 1847.

age in Erasmus's *Encomium Moriae*. The dialogue of Hiems and Ver is the antithesis of the whole action in *Love's Labor's Lost*; although it is rather cleaner and more coherent than similar songs of the period, it is written in a completely unassuming style, so close to that of the popular ditties that scholars are still unsure whether it is a version of a preexisting song. The looming tragedy of *Othello* is heightened by Desdemona's singing of a silly song of despised love, with a mildly ironic twist in its tail, and the traditional refrain, "Sing willow, willow, willow." The exiled princes' dirge for

Imogen in *Cymbeline* has caused furious head-scratching, although its sooth is a good deal less silly than Feste's.

The most inscrutable part of Shakespeare's artistic method is the degree to which he bases his work in folk entertainments, traditional festivals, and popular culture generally. Most of his educated contemporaries were too grand to compile records of the calendar of country amusements, which were probably multifarious and complicated; modern ethnography, which concerns itself with symbolic gestures and repeated motifs in popular pastime, had yet to be born. *The Winter's Tale* might give an idealized picture of a sheepshearing, but the symbolism of the celebration may be far more important to the play's structure than we can now realize. The shepherd, like Leontes, has lost a wife.

> . . . when my old wife liv'd, upon
> This day she was both pantler, butler, cook,
> Both dame and servant; welcom'd all, serv'd all;
> Would sing her song and dance her turn; now here
> At upper end o' th' table, now i' th' middle;
> On his shoulder, and his; her face o' fire
> With labor, and the thing she took to quench it
> She would to each one sip.

(4.4.55–62)

Leontes lost a wife because he misinterpreted the welcome she gave to his guest. The shepherd's innocent commentary on the main action has never been given any importance, although the sheepshearing is the heart of the play and Autolycus's assault on the gullibility of the shepherds one of its main sources of tension.

The Russian writer Leo Tolstoy (1828–1910), seen in this undated photograph, was not a fan of Shakespeare. Of *King Lear*, he said, "Far from being the height of perfection, it is a very bad, carelessly composed production, which . . . can not evoke among us anything but aversion and weariness."

In defending *King Lear* against Tolstoy's bitter condemnation, George Orwell is obliged to argue that Shakespeare is no thinker, but a word musician, seducing his hearers by "mere skill in placing one syllable beside another." In doing so he concedes too much, but the true corollary of his own observations is almost unthinkable.

Almost never does he put a subversive or skeptical remark into the mouth of a character likely to be identified with himself. Throughout his plays the acute social critics, the people who are not taken in by accepted fallacies, are buffoons, villains, lunatics or persons who are shamming insanity or in a state of violent hysteria. *Lear* is a play in which this tendency is well marked. It contains a great deal of veiled social criticism—a point Tolstoy misses—but it is all uttered by the Fool, by Edgar when he is pretending to be mad, or by Lear during his bouts of madness. In his sane moments Lear hardly ever makes an intelligent remark.

Orwell's notion of the characters Shakespeare was likely to be identified with is quite arbitrary. In the Sonnets, for example, Shakespeare places himself alongside the buffoons, the tongue-tied, like the curate in *Love's Labor's Lost*, and regrets his debasement as a public entertainer, especially when his is an art of necessity "made tongue-tied by authority."

In his 1947 pamphlet *Lear, Tolstoy, and the Fool*, British writer George Orwell (1903–50) defends Shakespeare as a justly admired and highly skilled playwright. He further observes, "Properly speaking, one cannot *answer* Tolstoy's attack. The interesting question is: Why did he make it?" Orwell appears at left in an undated photograph.

The persona likens himself to an "unperfect actor on the stage / Who with his fear is put beside his part" and confesses that he has made himself "a motley to the view," "Gor'd mine own thoughts, sold cheap what is most dear" (CX). He asks for pity, and for the beloved to upbraid Fortune on his behalf (CXI):

> The guilty goddess of my harmful deeds,
> That did not better for my life provide
> Than public means, which public manners breeds.
> Thence comes it that my name receives a brand;
> And almost thence my nature is subdu'd
> To what it works in, like the dyer's hand.

It is a consequence of the bardolatry that Tolstoy so deplores that Shakespeare's peasant origins have been devalued and some sacerdotal role assumed for him. His very invisibility may be a consequence of his social insignificance; his contemporaries may have dismissed him as contemptuously as the Countess Russell is said to have done, as "the man Shakespeare."

As another countess remarks in Wedekind's *Lulu*, it takes a monster to see what is monstrous in society. As a public entertainer, protected from prosecution as a rogue or mountebank only by the patronage of some dignitary, Shakespeare is quite likely to have identified and been identified with the characters that Orwell discounts. In deciding what is mad and what is sane, and what hysteria and what shammed madness, Orwell makes the kind of judgment that Shakespeare's art invalidates. Orwell thinks that from Shakespeare's writings it would be difficult to know that he had any religion—whereas in fact the placing of truth in the mouths of babes is one aspect of the Christian respect for all human life; that same profound feeling is what inspires us to protest loudly when health authorities take a mental defective off a dialysis machine because they consider his quality of life too low, in defiance of Christ's words in the Sermon on the Mount (Matthew 5:22). The ultimate effect of such belief is to challenge all forms of human pretension and all social inequality based upon it. As Isabel warns Angelo in *Measure for Measure*, the assumption of any kind of superiority, and especially the kind of moral ascendancy he himself presumes to possess, is folly.

> . . . man, proud man,
> Dress'd in a little brief authority,
> Most ignorant of what he's most assur'd—
> His glassy essence—like an angry ape
> Plays such fantastic tricks before high heaven
> As makes the angels weep . . .

> *(2.2.118–23)*

The theater image which Shakespeare uses so often as a figure of the created universe here takes on a new dimension; the player has no more understanding of the vast drama in which he recites his part than a performing animal in some human spectacle.

There is no dearth of Shakespearean characters ready to interpret the world to anyone who will listen, but to assume that any one of them is the repository of Shakespeare's own ideological certainties is to ignore the fundamental relevance of the theater paradigm. When Hamlet says "there is nothing either good or bad but thinking makes it so," he is making a Wittgensteinian point: the meaning of the spectacle is not what is said by any participant but what the auditor is capable of carrying away from the whole—Shakespeare's world plus his auditors' worlds make an infinite regression. Intellectual life in the Shakespearean mode is a never-ending learning process; each of the plays enacts the mental adventure of skepticism. If Tolstoy and Orwell can both doubt Shakespeare's stature as a thinker, they show themselves incapable of recognizing ideas that are not expounded in a systematic manner. While Wittgenstein is uncomfortable in Shakespeare's mental landscape, he has no doubt that such a thing exists and that its contours are impressive. Its true horizon is established by reference not to Christian dogma but to those values that will guide us on our course toward a just society whether Christian dogma survives or not.

SIX

Sociology

●

The Quality of Steadfastness

Most of Shakespeare's thinking in the theater is less abstract than the huge themes of *King Lear* but it is all consistent with the system of values that is adumbrated in that great tragedy. In the comedies, he came as close to exposition of a system of practical values as he could without creating characters to serve as mouthpieces for his own ideas. Those values were derived from the culture of his Warwickshire ilk and diverged significantly from the received ideas of both city and court. At the core of a coherent social structure as he viewed it lay marriage, which for Shakespeare is no mere comic convention but a crucial

In Shakespeare's *Cymbeline*, the princess Imogen remains steadfastly devoted to her husband, Posthumus, through thick and thin. This photograph of the actress Ellen Terry (1847–1928) as Imogen was taken around 1899.

and complex ideal. He rejected the stereotype of the passive, sexless, unresponsive female and its inevitable concomitant, the misogynist conviction that all women were whores at heart. Instead he created a series of female characters who were both passionate and pure, who gave their hearts spontaneously into the keeping of the men they loved and remained true to the bargain in the face of tremendous odds. The women's steadfastness is in direct relation to their aggressiveness; the only Shakespearean woman to swerve from her commitment is Cressida, the passive manipulator of male desire and dissimulator of her own.

In rural households marriage was a partnership, involving hard physical labor on the part of the wife, as well as mutual forbearance in the long series of tribulations and reverses which country households had to survive.

> When all aloud the wind doth blow,
>> And coughing drowns the parson's saw,
> And birds sit brooding in the snow,
>> And Marian's nose looks red and raw,
> When roasted crabs hiss in the bowl,
> Then nightly sings the staring owl,
>> Tu-whit;
> Tu-who, a merry note,
> While greasy Joan doth keel the pot.

There can be no starker contrast to the ornate dalliance of the young lords in *Love's Labor's Lost* than the rustic song that replaces it on the stage (5.2.904–21), described by an unnamed commentator as the harsh words of Mercury in place of the songs of Apollo. The inference is clear: lovemaking is easy when the fields are full of flowers and the girls sweet-smelling in freshly bleached linens, but marriages are made when the owl, Minerva's bird, makes its melancholy call from the dark fields and all must huddle round the smoky fire. The winter of the year is also a figure of the winter of human life, when love has to ripen into friendship and tolerance, regardless of the unsightliness of Marian's chapped face and Joan's ropy hair.

When Sly, the drunken tinker, is taken up by the lord's retinue in the Induction to *The Taming of the Shrew*, he is given a wife and told how to treat her in the manner befitting one of his rank, but he proves strangely recalcitrant. When the disguised page comes before him as his wife, "she" abases herself. Sly answers:

> Are you my wife, and will not call me husband?
> My men should call me "lord," I am your goodman.
>
> *(Induction, 2.105–6)*

When told he must call her "madam," he insists on calling her by name, "Alice madam or Joan madam," only to be instructed to address her as "Madam and nothing else, so lords call ladies" (112). But he can only manage to call her "madam wife," and asks her to sit by his side "and let the world slip." *The Taming of the Shrew* is not a knockabout farce of wife-battering, but the cunning adaptation of a folk-motif to show the forging of a partnership between equals. Petruchio is not looking to fall in love, but to find a wife. His choice is based on self-interest in that he must find a woman who has some property of her own and who can help to run the estate he has just inherited. He chooses Kate as he would a horse, for her high mettle, and he must use at least as much intelligence and energy in bringing her to trust him, and to accept the bargain he offers, as he would in breaking a horse. The image can be found in Aristotle, Socrates, Xenophon, Plutarch, and Cato, but Shakespeare's use of it comes from the same imaginative context that fashioned the steadfast, straightforward wives of Windsor.

Nowadays we have largely accepted the ideal of marriage which chooses a Beatrice for a Benedick, but the notion of egalitarian marriage was far from universal in Shakespeare's day, especially among the literate classes. In his early comedies he went to uncharacteristic lengths to provide clear exempla of the kind of relationship he saw as producing an appropriate outcome for a comedy. In *The Comedy of Errors* he constructs three perspectives from which to view the achievement of a marriage: the overview

in the story of Egeon and Emilia, the courting stage in Antipholus of Syracuse and Luciana, and its consequence in the disappointment of Adriana and the estrangement of Antipholus of Ephesus from her.

The Comedy of Errors is based on the *Menaechmi* of Plautus, but the main action is encased in the arching plot, which describes how Egeon was separated from his wife when their ship split and "her part was carried with more speed before the wind." Unless he can find money to redeem his life, he will have to die at the end of the day. To an audience familiar with Terentian comedy, this means that he has the play time in which to find and reconstitute his broken family. Salvation is

This engraving of a scene from *The Taming of the Shrew* depicts Petruchio as he rejects a gown he had ordered for Kate because he deems it to be of inferior quality, despite the fact that Kate likes it. (The cap on the floor met with the same fate.) In this and many other ways, Petruchio, as he would with a valuable animal, gradually "trains" Kate to trust him. W. Thomas's engraving, after a painting by Charles Robert Leslie (1794–1859), was sold as a print in the London *Evening News*.

signaled by the finding of lost children both in *Pericles* and *The Winter's Tale*, written as close to the end of Shakespeare's career as *The Comedy of Errors* is to the beginning, while the reunion of separated man and wife furnishes the comic catastrophe in *All's Well That Ends Well*, *Cymbeline*, and *The Winter's Tale*. The later treatments are more romantic, the practical applications less obvious, but all project the same idea of marriage as a heroic way of life, in which the pleasures of propinquity are not the essential element.

In *The Comedy of Errors* the wife who reappears to resolve the confusion of the Antipholi and save her husband is an Abbess; her words have the priestly ring of absolution:

> Whoever bound him, I will loose his bonds,
> And gain a husband by his liberty.

(5. 1. 339–40)

Hermione, in *The Winter's Tale*, by a living death similar to the Abbess's renunciation of public life, expiates her husband's crimes of jealousy. It has been objected that the Shakespearean stereotype of the redemptive woman is passive and that he is doing no more than upholding the double standard of sexual morality. The truth is more complex and more interesting. The Abbess is no cipher but a figure of power in Ephesus. Hermione is not rejected by her husband, who repents when he learns of the oracle and of his son's death as foretold by it. Rather, she refuses to live by his side in a tainted union and chooses to be buried alive, as it were, for sixteen years. Helena, in *All's Well That Ends Well*, undertakes a daring enterprise in order to be entitled to the husband of her choice, and then forces consummation of their union by becoming a camp-follower and conceiving his child against his will, under the guise of fornication.

It must be remembered that while Shakespeare's concept of virtue tends to the active rather than the contemplative, his view of redemptive action is Christian. Christ, the paradigm for both men and women, redeemed humanity by suffering and dying on the cross. The Christian concept of passive heroism places a high value on endurance, which in Shakespeare's ethic is cognate with constancy and hence with truth (see Sonnets CXVI and CXIX). While he may make reference to a contemporary stereotype of women as fickle as in Sonnet XX, and allows both Isabel and Viola to animadvert on women's malleability, of all Shakespeare's plays only *Troilus and Cressida* deals with a genuine case of female treachery. The theme is mainly demonstrated as a constant male preoccupation, for Frank Ford in *The Merry Wives of Windsor*, Claudio in *Much Ado*, Posthumus in *Cymbeline*, Othello, and Leontes in *The Winter's Tale* all err in not trusting their wives. While female characters, having spontaneously and often suddenly committed themselves to a man, never swerve from the commitment, though in respecting it they may be called upon to risk their lives, Shakespeare's male characters, among them Proteus, Valentine, Orsino, Romeo, and Angelo, will break vows and transfer their affections in no longer than it takes to tell. Shakespeare seems to agree with Hermia in *A Midsummer Night's Dream* that men have broken more vows than women have ever spoken (1.1.175–76). The inconstancy of men causes no great upheaval in the Shakespeare world, but when the solidity and truth of women are undermined, as in *Titus Andronicus, Troilus and Cressida*, and *King Lear*, the world regresses to savagery.

Shakespeare did not think of constancy as a psychosexual characteristic allied to masochism, but rather as an earthly manifestation of divine love, which is beyond gender. The turtledove in "The Phoenix and the Turtle" is both a figure of constancy and male. The persona of the Sonnets cannot escape from his love vassalage, regardless of his beloved's perfidy, despite separation, calumny, public humiliation, and even the beloved's promiscuity and withdrawal of affection. Although he may permit himself ironies and denigrations, Shakespeare's persona continues to project the ideal of diamond-hard constancy, beyond death and dishonor, in despite of all treachery. In his acts of submission, he outdoes any wife in the canon:

> That god forbid, that made me first your slave.
> I should in thought control your times of pleasure,
> Or at your hand th'account of hours to crave,
> Being your vassal bound to stay your leisure!
> Oh, let me suffer, being at your beck,
> Th'imprison'd absence of your liberty,
> And patience, tame to sufferance, bide each check
> Without accusing you of injury.
> Be where you list; your charter is so strong
> That you yourself may privilege your time
> To what you will; to you it doth belong
> Your self to pardon of self-doing crime.
> I am to wait, though waiting so be hell,
> Not blame your pleasure, be it ill or well.

(Sonnet LVIII)

Courtship: Ideal and Reality

The Abbess of *The Comedy of Errors* has waited out her thirty-three-year separation in perfect celibacy. Shakespeare places a high value upon chastity, but he does not go so far as some of his contemporaries who thought that virtuous women had no physical desires. His witty ladies

Courtly conventions of romance were, for Shakespeare, a devious and self-deceiving way to disguise our basic physical desires. This miniature by the British artist Nicholas Hilliard (1547–1619) evokes the stereotype of the lovesick swain whose melancholy posturing characterized so much of the love poetry of the time. Some scholars believe the man depicted in the painting is Robert Devereux, second Earl of Essex, a favorite of Queen Elizabeth I.

swap bawdy *doubles entendres* with each other and with men, without sacrificing any of their own integrity. In *Romeo and Juliet*, a lover who has been content to languish in correct Petrarchan fashion for Rosaline finds himself whisked off to church and bedded by the child Juliet, who, unlike Rosaline, has no cunning to be strange. Mercutio celebrates the restoration achieved by requited love:

Why, is not this better now than groaning for love? Now art thou
sociable, now art thou Romeo; now art thou what thou art, by art as
well as by nature. For this driveling love is like a great natural that
runs lolling up and down to hide his bauble in a hole.

(2.4.88–93)

Mercutio implies that all the extravagant posturing of courtly love
hides a simple human urge to copulate. In *The Two Gentlemen of Verona*,
Sylvia is celebrated with all the hyperbole of debased Petrarchism.

Who is Sylvia? What is she
That all our swains commend her?
Holy, fair, and wise is she,
The heaven such grace did lend her,
    That she might admired be.

(4.2.38–42)

Valentine "sells" Sylvia to Proteus, insisting that she is a "heavenly saint,"
demanding that he "call her divine,"

    . . . if not divine,
Yet let her be a principality,
Sovereign to all the creatures on the earth.

(2.4.146–48)

Her "worth makes other worthies nothing: / She is alone" (2 4.161–62).
    This is the highest Platonic praise. Such praise attributes to the
beloved the ultimate perfection of the Form of Forms, comprehending all.

It is not surprising that Proteus's hometown sweetheart fades in his memory. As he explains,

> At first I did adore a twinkling star,
> But now I worship a celestial sun . . .
>
> *(2.6.9–10)*

The sun as principal light of the world is itself a figure of the divinity; we can find hundreds of similar uses in Petrarch's *Canzoniere* and in the imagery used by Dante in describing Beatrice. Bedazzled as he may be, in act 4, scene 4, Proteus translates his poetic brainstorm into an unceremonious rape attempt.

Antipholus of Syracuse in *The Comedy of Errors* extravagantly humbles himself before Luciana, in a rhymed speech full of Ovidian echoes and pseudo-Platonic themes:

> Teach me, dear creature, how to think and speak;
> Lay open to my earthy gross conceit . . .
> The folded meaning of your words' deceit . . .
> Are you a god? would you create me new?
> Transform me then, and to your power I'll yield.
>
> *(3.2.33–34, 36, 39–40)*

Here Shakespeare is mocking the debased tradition by using images from the *Metamorphoses* as ironic comments on the way men lose their angelic capacity of reason in the quest for amorous gratification, just as the gods took on the characters of beasts. Lucentio compares Bianca to Europa (and himself, by extension, to a horned beast).

The Elizabethans did not consider amorousness a particularly masculine characteristic. From being baby and schoolboy, in Jaques's scenario, a man goes on to play the lover "sighing like furnace, with a woeful ballad / Made to his mistress' eyebrow." The stereotype can be found too in the interlude *Mundus et Infans*: the teenage boy is typified as "Lust and Liking," until he qualifies for knight service at twenty-one and becomes "Manhood Mighty." We are not surprised to find a tradition of vilifying lovesickness among the schoolmen whose charges were most susceptible to it. Erasmus castigates "this pangue or guierie of love" which "dooeth especially above all others, invade and possesse suche persons as be altogether drouned in idlenesse." Lucentio, in Padua to study Aristotelian philosophy at the university (1. 1. 17–20), falls prey to it in *The Taming of the Shrew*:

> . . . while idly I stood looking on,
> I found the effect of love in idleness . . .

(1.1.150–51)

So he undertakes the conquest of Bianca, assuming the identity of his servant, producing a spurious father, almost disowning his own, only to find in Petruchio's demonstration that his wife is more than he can handle.

In England in the 1590s poetical lovemaking seems to have become a kind of epidemic. Young men, stuffed with "taffeta phrases, silken terms precise," used them to turn the heads of silly women, disrupting the orderly progress of their courtship by humbler swains. Twice Elizabeth enacted severe penalties for the stealing of heiresses by the kinds of means deplored by Egeus in *Midsummer Night's Dream*:

Thou, thou, Lysander, thou hast given her rhymes,
And interchang'd love-tokens with my child:
Thou hast by moonlight at her window sung
With faining voice verses of feigning love,
And stol'n the impression of her fantasy
With bracelets of thy hair, rings, gauds, conceits,
Knacks, trifles, nosegays, sweetmeats (messengers
Of strong prevailment in unharden'd youth):
With cunning hast thou filch'd my daughter's heart . . .

(1.1.28–36)

Moth, the wise little page in *Love's Labor's Lost*, utters a swingeing condemnation of love *à la mode*:

to jig off a tune at the tongue's end, canary to it with your feet, humor it with turning up your eyelids, sigh a note and sing a note, sometime through the throat as if you swallowed love with singing love, sometime through the nose as if you snuffed up love by smelling love; with your hat penthouse-like o'er the shop of your eyes; with your arms crossed on your thin-belly doublet like a rabbit on a spit; or your hands in your pocket like a man after the old painting; and keep not too long in one tune, but a snip, and away. These are complements, these are humors, these betray nice wenches, that would be betrayed without these; and make them men of note (do you note, men?) that most are affected to these.

(3.1.9–23)

Moth implies that the affectations of such lovers as he describes are only likely to be effective with women who are easy or, in Elizabethan parlance, "light." Armado succeeds in seducing Jaquenetta, to be sure, but Jaquenetta is a silly country girl who has no defense against him. The young lords accost the ladies of France with more evolved versions of the same convention, but the ladies treat the whole business as a game, and a rather narcissistic and misconceived game at that. None of Shakespeare's

The mock marriage between Rosalind and Orlando that takes place in Act 4, scene 1, of *As You Like It* is depicted in this 1853 painting by Walter Howell Deverell. In this case, the female figure is not the bride but Celia acting as the priest. Both bride and groom in the mock ceremony are supposed to be male.

comic heroines is won in a love game of this kind. Sylvia, Portia, and Olivia preempt courtship by generously committing themselves. Rosalind/Ganymede and Viola/Cesario earn love by concealing their femininity and thereby escaping the courtship process. In this genderless (but not sexless) guise, they can express their own versions of Moth's contempt. As Ganymede Rosalind can put a stop to Orlando's conventional pursuit, which mainly consists in disfiguring trees with bad poetry, not merely by mocking the stereotype of love melancholy but by enacting a marriage ceremony before the courtship is well under way.

Rosalind's bitter remark, "men are April when they woo, December when they wed. Maids are May when they are maids, but the sky changes when they are wives" (*As You Like It*, 4.1.139–41), could be construed in terms of the device of the two Antipholi in *The Comedy of Errors*: Shakespeare gives many clues in the imagery of the water drops (1.2.35–40) and of time running backward (4.2.53–62) to suggest that the two are in fact identical, and separated only by the pulse of time which has moved faster for Antipholus of Syracuse than it has for his brother. Antipholus of Ephesus is no longer May but December, no longer "Lust and Liking" like his milder, more pliable brother, but "sudden and quick in quarrel." Neither version can see himself in the other; Antipholus of Syracuse cannot deal with his brother's problem or recognize it as potentially his own. Within the arching plot which projects an image of the spiritual value of the ideal married state, Shakespeare has provided a split image of the reality which begins in the maygame of dalliance and is lived out in the stress and strain of mutual disappointment.

It must not be thought that the author of "The Phoenix and the Turtle" rejected the ideal of Platonic love. Rather he understood, as few

English poets of his time understood, that the ideal is an ideal and not a vehicle for mundane desires, whether for catamite, concubine, or wife. The identification of lover and beloved is not something experienced every day but an aspect of the spiritual relationship between them. Just as Adriana in *The Comedy of Errors* cannot expect to act out her bond with her husband, cannot merge with him and become in this life one flesh, the Platonic lover is so by virtue of his commitment, not by physical intimacy. The amorousness of youth has little to do with the desire for the union of souls; what Shakespeare mocks time and again is the borrowing of the imagery of the union of souls for something far more immediate and specific and transitory.

The Achievement of Marriage

For Shakespeare marriage was not simply a cliché for ending the action, although it became so in his lifetime. He was profoundly interested in the paradox of creating a durable social institution out of the volatile material of lovers' fantasies. In *Midsummer Night's Dream*, the lovers' broil is first complicated and then sorted out by fairy magic, which merges into ritual, which alone can reconcile Diana, goddess of chastity and childbirth, and Venus, the equally indispensable avatar of sexual attraction, who have been poised against each other in equal combat throughout the play.

Romeo and Juliet offers us the tragic counterpart of the same idea. In the sick society of Verona, the love of two young people who are otherwise perfectly matched is turned to disaster. There is more wrong with Verona than the senseless feud "bred of an airy word." The matter of Juliet's age takes twenty-five lines to tell, and is repeated three times; her mother tells us that she bore Juliet at the same age, making her

In act 2, scene 6, of *Romeo and Juliet*, the young lovers are married in secret by the sympathetic Friar Lawrence, an event that takes place offstage. This photograph shows the actors Vernon Steel as Romeo, Phyllis Neilson-Terry as Juliet, and J. Fisher-White as Friar Lawrence in a 1911 production of the play at the New Theatre in London.

twenty-eight. Later we hear from her husband that he has not danced since before his wife was born. The matter is not so stressed because it is what Elizabethan audiences would take for granted, but because it is not. Juliet's youth, and the general distortion of mores in a society which married children to old men, is an important aspect of the tragedy. In devoting herself to Romeo Juliet takes an irrevocably tragic step; she has to teach him the accents of true love, which in the balcony scene she does by silencing him whenever he embarks on one of the set speeches he would have used on Rosaline. Friar Lawrence chides Romeo for his fickleness, and justifies Rosaline's coldness:

> O, she knew well
> Thy love did read by rote that could not spell.

(2.3.83–84)

Juliet loves with the full power of her innocence; in cobbling a clandestine marriage between the warring houses, Friar Lawrence makes her a martyr to the corruption of Verona. Her father's attitude—"And you be mine I'll give you to my friend"—is clearly wrong.

Oceans of ink were spilled in England during the turmoil of the Reformation over the status of the married life, the rights of lovers, and the interest of parents in their children's matings. The consensus was that parents did indeed have some say in how their children disposed of themselves, but no parent could force a child to marry against its will or refuse a match which was otherwise suitable. In such cases the children could have redress to the ecclesiastical authorities. The common people were scandalized by the dynastic marriages arranged by the nobility who disposed of their children, according to the religious polemicists, as if they had been so many cattle and sheep, especially when so many of the marriages with wards of the Crown later came to violent or adulterous ends. In treating the issue so seriously, Shakespeare was giving form to the Protestant ideology of marriage, as it is movingly expressed in *The Golden Boke of Christen Matrimonye* (1542):

> Let other set forth syngle lyvynge with so many prayses . . . yet wyll
> I for evermore commend the state of honorable wedlocke, which

refuseth no kynde of payne and trouble so that yt may brynge any profite at all to the publique weal of Christendome . . . yet wyll I preferre that state of lyvynge whiche accordynge to the order of charite, is redy at all times to beare the burden of other, and to seke the quietnes of other, no lesse then of it selfe.

The Protestant reformers believed with utter seriousness that husbands and wives could and should help each other to heaven; ill-assorted unions on the other hand were a diurnal occasion of grave sin. In *The Merry Wives of Windsor*, Master Fenton justifies his elopement with Ann Page on the grounds of her parents' guilt:

You would have married her most shamefully,
Where there was no proportion held in love.
The truth is, she and I, long since contracted,
Are now so sure that nothing can dissolve us . . .
    . . . therein she does evitate and shun
A thousand irreligious cursed hours
Which forced marriage would have brought upon her.

(5.5218–21, 225–27)

The marriages of Ford and Page demonstrate what "proportion held in love" leads to; they have the usual problems of disagreement (as well as a rather unusual degree of paranoia in the case of Ford) but the solidity of the spouses' commitment is never in doubt. The wives enjoy the freedom which was so envied by their Continental counterparts because of the freely given trust of their husbands, which in the course of the shaming of the lecherous Falstaff they show that they thoroughly deserve.

One of the chief pitfalls on the way to achieving the Protestant ideal was the possibility of the clandestine wedding. The ministers of the sacrament of matrimony are the man and woman; no other witness except God was required. The clergyman participates in marriages chiefly as a witness. In Elizabethan England, the words of espousal were sufficient to bind man and woman together irrevocably in the eyes of God; any subsequent marriage, no matter how formally celebrated, could be invalidated merely on the plea of prior contract. In *As You Like It*, Touchstone woos Audrey in much the same vein as Armado wooed Jaquenetta, and finds a hedgepriest to marry them. The priest jibs at the lack of someone to give the bride away, and Jaques steps forward, but instead of playing his part, turns on Touchstone:

> And will you, being a man of your breeding, be married under a bush like a beggar? Get you to church, and have a good priest that can tell you what marriage is. This fellow will but join you together as they join wainscot; then one of you will prove a shrunk panel, and like green timber, warp, warp.

> (3.3.74–80)

Touchstone's aside proves the truth of Jaques's observation: "I am not in the mind but I were better to be married of him than of another, for he is not like to marry me well; and not being well married, it will be a good excuse for me hereafter to leave my wife" (3.3.81–85).

This aborted marriage has its parallel in the mock marriage between the disguised Rosalind and Orlando, in which Celia plays the hedgepriest. Rosalind corrects her on a tickle point—if the words of espousal are said in the wrong tense, the marriage is not marriage but trothplight.

ROS: You must begin, "Will you Orlando—"

CEL: Go to. Will you Orlando have to wife this Rosalind?

ORL: I will.

ROS: Ay, but when?

ORL: Why now, as fast as she can marry us.

ROS: Then you must say "I take thee Rosalind for wife."

ORL: I take thee Rosalind for wife.

ROS: I might ask you for your commission: but I do take thee Orlando for my husband.

(4.1.122–31)

It is important in understanding *As You Like It* that Orlando be seen and heard to marry Rosalind in her boy's disguise, even though in canon law the fact that one party is disguised would invalidate the contract.

In marriage, sexual attraction (which is not necessarily absent from Orlando's relation with a pretty boy, or Orsino's either for that matter) is overshadowed by friendship and general compatibility. A husband was more than a lover; in the words of *The Bride's Goodmorrow*, one of the best known of Elizabethan ballads, a husband was

> . . . a friend for to defend you
>> From sorrow care and smart.
> In health and sickness, for thy comfort day and night
>> He is approved and brought,
> Whose love and liking is most constant sure and right;
>> Then love him as ye ought.
> There is no treasure which may be compared
>> Unto a faithful friend.

Gold soon decayeth and worldly wealth consumeth
>And wasteth in the wind:
But love, once planted in a pure and perfect mind,
>Endureth weal and woe;
The frowns of fortune, come they ne'er so unkind
>Cannot the same o'erthrow.

We have become so used to marriage as a central theme for serious literature that it is not easy for us to estimate Shakespeare's originality

Around 1580, the Flemish artist Jan van der Straet published his influential *Nova Reperta*, or New Discoveries—a collection of twenty-four engravings depicting the technological and geographical advances of the time. This scene, engraved by Philip Galle after van der Straet's drawing, depicts workers operating a printing press.

in developing the idea of the complementary couple as the linchpin of the social structure. The medieval Church regarded marriage as a second-rate condition, inferior both to virginity and celibacy, and to widowhood. Fraternal association was stressed at the expense of heterosexual commitment and intimacy, and one-sex hierarchy remained the pattern of social institutions. Shakespeare was writing after generations of religious upheaval in the course of which the hierarchical religious establishment had had to face a determined onslaught from champions of a more populist religion which drew very different lessons from the scriptures and demanded the right to follow the dictates of individual conscience.

However they might differ on other issues, all the reformers vigorously defended the honourable estate of matrimony. In developing the character of Portia in *The Merchant of Venice*, for instance, Shakespeare used an existent motif, but his invention of the casket plot, so finely poised on the question of fathers' rights and heiresses' vulnerability, takes us through the whole development of a marriage relationship in a way that is profoundly original—it is because it has been so influential that it has come to seem to us utterly conventional.

The growth and development of the printing industry both stimulated and fed the desire for literacy. As literacy spread from above, social ideals seeped into literature from below. Straddling both written and verbal forms as a writer for the theater, Shakespeare took up the cudgels on the side of the reformers, giving charm and life to their sometimes strident convictions. He projected the ideal of the monogamous heterosexual couple so luminously in his matings that they irradiate our notions of compatibility and cooperation between spouses to this day. Academic comedy has little to do with women and nothing to do with wooing; sophisticated Continental comedy dealt principally with adulterous intrigue or stereotyped matings impeded by other plot contingencies. The ancestors of Beatrice and Benedick are probably to be found in the unwritten lore of the common people, which Shakespeare may have absorbed even more efficiently than he did the commonplaces of academic and courtly literature. Shakespeare imposed no exclusive criteria upon his vocabulary and erected no shibboleth of purity of diction, such as was to hamstring Continental theater for centuries. Dialect and jargon words were all grist to his voracious mill, laying the ground for an unrivalled linguistic heritage. His attitude was profoundly pragmatic; he took what was there, without troubling to consider whether it should have been there or not. Because he imposed no *post hoc* system upon the multifariousness of his experience and based his utterance upon what could be comprehended and registered in the conditions of dramatic representation, his work continues to breathe—its audience gives it lungs. To argue thus is not to argue, as Orwell did, that Shakespeare's work contains no thought at all. Rather its pragmatism is part of its thought; each theatrical exposure is a kind of experiment. The characters and their discourse are thrown together in the crucible; the resulting compound is what the audience carries away. It may not be possible to extract a nugget of thought, which we usually think of as a series of interrelated propositions, but part of the reason for that is that Shakespeare knew, as we have forgotten, that feeling is as intellectual as thinking. His is, as Eliot would argue, an intact nondissociative sensibility. The Shakespearean idea is inseparable from the mode of its expression.

As long as Shakespeare remains central to English cultural life, it will retain the values which make it unique in the world, namely tolerance, pluralism, the talent for viable compromise, and a profound commitment to that most wasteful form of social organization, democracy. To an outsider such lack of system may seem amorphous, disorganized, and even hypocritical; from within it is evident that such an inclusive mode can be no more inconsistent than life itself. The puzzle is to discover the intrinsic ordering principle in apparent disorder. Perhaps the reason the principle eludes so many is that they are searching in the wrong place; in the theater the beholder is the medium. The missing middle term in the Shakespearean proposition is our response. Without that there is and can be no argument.

NOTE ON SOURCES

·

The verse quoted at the end of the section "Shakespeare's 'Honest Mirth' " in Chapter 2 is from Nicholas Udall's *Ralph Roister Doister* (published ca. 1560). The quotations from Wittgenstein which conclude Chapters 2 and 3 are taken from *Vermischte Bemerkungen*, translated by Peter Winch (Blackwell, 1980). The first is dated 1949 and the second 1939–40. Thomas Nashe's reference to *Henry IV Part I* at the beginning of Chapter 4 is from *Pierce Pennilesse His Supplication to the Divell* (1592). The verse by Sir John Davies quoted at the end of Chapter 4 is from *Orchestra* (1596). George Orwell's remarks quoted on pages 151–52 are taken from "Lear, Tolstoy, and the Fool," in his *Critical Essays* (1946). Erasmus's castigation of lovesickness on page 168 is cited from his *Apothegmes*, translated by Nicholas Udall (1542).

FURTHER READING

•

Two studies, both published in the same year, may help to elucidate the rather complex argument adumbrated in these pages. One is an essay by L. C. Knights, published in O. Johnson (ed.), *The Hidden Harmony: Essays in Honor of Philip Wheelwright* (New York, 1967), called "The Thought of Shakespeare," in which he argues that the concept "thought" needs to be redefined in order to comprehend Shakespeare's way of developing ideas in the theater. The other is Norman Rabkin's *Shakespeare and the Common Understanding* (New York, 1967), which makes a related point at greater length. However, it should be obvious that the best further reading is Shakespeare's work itself, preferably in a fully annotated version, such as in the Methuen New Arden editions of the individual plays, which offer the possibility of comparing Shakespeare's treatment with his sources, so that the nature of the controlling imagination can be recognized at first hand. The quality of the individual editions is not uniform, however, and readers may find that they must consult other editions, such as the Oxford Shakespeare or even the earlier Arden ones.

Reading Shakespeare in the study can be misleading, for it encourages the picking out of a single strand of his complex mimetic arguments at the cost of the whole. The answer is not simply to attend performances of the plays, which are nowadays highly "interpretive," full of distracting stage business and elaborate and irrelevant characterization, so that the language is difficult to hear and to follow, but to read the plays in groups. Paradoxically, a "bad" performance, such as might be expected from schoolchildren, is sometimes the most illuminating.

There have been few systematic attempts to extrapolate Shakespeare's philosophy from his work. The most authoritative is still W. C. Curry, *Shakespeare's Philosophical Patterns* (Baton Rouge, La., 1937), but readers may well find John Erskine Hankins, *Backgrounds of Shakespeare's Thought* (Hassocks, 1978), more useful. For more committed students, the bibliography edited by W. R. Elton, *Shakespeare's World: Renaissance Intellectual Contexts, A Selective Annotated Guide 1966–71* (Garland, 1979), is indispensable. A brief but elegant discussion by J. W. Lever, "Shakespeare and the Ideas of His Time," can be found in the *Shakespeare Survey* for 1976.

The indisputable facts of Shakespeare's life can be found in S. Schoenbaum, *Shakespeare: A Documentary Life* (Oxford, 1975), while the classic studies by W. W. Greg, *The Editorial Problem in Shakespeare* (Oxford, 1942), and E. K. Chambers, *Shakespeare: A Study of Pacts and Problems* (Oxford, 1930), will help with interpretation in detail of the texts as we have them. Background study of Shakespeare's audience, crucial to this kind of analysis, is virtually nonexistent, but readers may find illuminating J. D. Wilson, *Life in Shakespeare's England* (New York, 1944), F. P. Wilson, *The Plague in Shakespeare's London* (Oxford, 1927); and of course E. K. Chambers, *The Elizabethan Stage* (Oxford, 1923).

The most useful gloss to the "Poetics" chapter must be Gregory Smith's edition of *Elizabethan Critical Essays* (Oxford, 1904), buttressed by Marvin T. Herrick, *The Poetics of Aristotle in England* (New Haven,

Conn., 1930). Alvin Kernan, "Shakespeare's Essays on Dramatic Poetry: The Nature and Function of Theater Within the Sonnets and the Plays," in a collection edited by Louis L. Martz and Aubrey Williams, *The Author in His Work: A Problem in Criticism* (New Haven, Conn., and London, 1978), discusses the fact that each of the plays which have totally invented plots, *Love's Labor's Lost, A Midsummer Night's Dream,* and *The Tempest,* is preoccupied with questions of dramatic form. A recent study of the centrality of the idea of theater in Shakespeare, *Player King and Adversary: Two Faces of Play in Shakespeare* (Baton Rouge, La., 1980), by E. J. Allman, develops the argument broached by James Winny in *The Player King: A Theme of Shakespeare's Histories* (New York, 1970). Anne Righter (Barton), *Shakespeare and the Idea of the Play* (Cambridge, 1962), is still stimulating. The connections with modern dramaturgy are explored by H. Felperin, *Shakespearean Representation: Mimesis and Modernity in Elizabethan Tragedy* (Princeton, 1978).

Basic works of reference for Shakespeare's ethics include T. W. Baldwin, *Shakespeare's "Small Latine and Lesse Greeke"* (Urbana, Ill., 1944), R. Noble, *Shakespeare's Biblical Knowledge,* and A. Hart, *Shakespeare and the Homilies* (Melbourne, 1934). Readers may find R. M. Frye, *Shakespeare and Christian Doctrine* (Princeton, 1963), affords a useful overview, and some of my own views expounded more rigorously in Bernard Spivack, *Shakespeare and the Allegory of Evil* (New York, 1958).

It is impossible to investigate Shakespeare's politics without coming up against E. M. W. Tillyard's immensely influential *The Elizabethan World Picture* (London, 1943), which needs to be balanced by a recognition of the progressive elements in Renaissance thought, perhaps as described in Q. Skinner, *Foundations of Modern Political Thought* (Cambridge, 1979). Both Tillyard's *Shakespeare's History Plays* (London, 1944) and Lily B. Campbell, *Shakespeare's Histories* (San Marino, 1947), are useful, and Irving Ribner in *The English History Play in the Age of Shakespeare* (Princeton, 1957) supplies a wider context. A full development of the idea of *theatrum mundi* can be found in Frances Yates, *Theater of the World* (London, 1971), while A. R. Humphreys's British Academy Lecture, *Shakespeare's Histories and "The Emotion of Multitude"* (Oxford, 1968), discusses the importance of audience self-awareness, also developed in *The Triple Bond* (Philadelphia, 1975), a collection of essays edited by J. G. Price. Those intrigued by the idea of "paraconsistent logic" might like to pursue it via a survey article by A. I. Arruda, to be found in A. I. Arruda, R. Chuaqui, and N. C. A. Da Costa (eds.), *Mathematical Logic in Latin America* (Hilversum, 1980).

A useful source for Shakespeare's teleology is R. H. Popkin, *The History of Skepticism from Erasmus to Descartes* (Assen, 1964). Discussions of Shakespeare's mental landscape are usually undertaken by littérateurs who hesitate, with reason, before plunging into the history of ideas. Some valuable insights can be found in H. Haydn, *The Counter-Renaissance* (New York, 1950), D. G. James, *The Dream of Learning* (Oxford, 1951), H. Craig, *The Enchanted Glass* (New York, 1936), Theodore Spencer, *Shakespeare and the Nature of Man* (Cambridge, 1942), J. F. Danby, *Shakespeare's Doctrine of Nature* (London, 1949), and latterly John Bayley, *The Uses of Division* (London, 1976), while A. O. Lovejoy, *The Great Chain of Being* (Cambridge, Mass., 1936), still exerts its charm.

Demographic history is still an infant study; a really authoritative study of marriage in Shakespeare's England has yet to be written, but students may find helpful an article by G. R. Hibbard, "Love, Marriage, and Money in Shakespeare's Theater and Shakespeare's England," in volume 6 (1978) of *The Elizabethan Theater* (ed. G. R. Hibbard).

Our understanding of the importance of the popular tradition is advanced somewhat by Robert Weimann, *Shakespeare and the Popular Tradition in the Theater: Studies in the Social Dimension of Dramatic Form and Function* (Baltimore and London, 1978), but pioneering studies like S. L. Bethell, *Shakespeare and the Popular Dramatic Tradition* (Westminster, 1944), and Louis B. Wright, *Middle Class Culture in Elizabethan England* (Chapel Hill, N.C., 1935), are still useful. The best discussion of the multiple function of cross-sex disguising is probably Nancy K. Hales's essay in the *Shakespeare Survey* for 1979, "Sexual Disguise in *As You Like It* and *Twelfth Night*." H. M. Richmond, *Shakespeare's Sexual Comedy: A Mirror for Lovers* (New York and Indiana, 1973), addresses related issues. Readers who are interested in a more detailed exposition of my own views on the subject may consult my Ph.D. thesis, "The Ethic of Love and Marriage in Shakespeare's Early Comedies" (1967), in Cambridge University Library.

More Further Reading

In the years since the above introduction to Shakespeare's thought was written, the literary industry surrounding the bard has produced its usual spate of publications. At present there are available more than nine thousand items in print and other media. Most of these are editions of the plays singly or in groups or in collected editions, with commentaries and guides for students at all levels; others are companions to the works, children's versions, cribs, glossaries, discussions of Shakespearean productions in all the countries of the world and of Shakespeare on film. The plays have been mined for all kinds of valuable nuggets to make up Shakespearean manuals of self-improvement, leadership, business, and management. Relatively little has addressed the five areas broached in my discussion and none of it would displace any of the titles I have cited above. Schoenbaum is still the authority on Shakespeare's life, and a paperback version of his *Documentary Life* is available. To it might profitably be added Peter Thomson's *Shakespeare's Professional Career* (Cambridge, 1999). An entertaining and beautifully illustrated introduction is Jean-Pierre Laroque's *Shakespeare, Court, Crowd, and Playhouse* (London, 1993).

Serious discussions of Shakespeare's thought are few; stimulating and contradictory accounts may be found in the collection of essays edited by John J. Joughin, under the title *Philosophical Shakespeares* (London, 2000).

Pauline Kiernan's *Shakespeare's Theory of Drama* (Cambridge, 1996) and Louis Montrose's *The Purpose of Playing: Shakespeare and the Cultural Politics of the Elizabethan Theater* (Chicago, 1996) deal in different ways with the didactic aesthetic of Shakespeare's theater. Valuable insights into Shakespeare's aesthetics are provided by Brian Gibbons in *Shakespeare and Multiplicity* (Cambridge, 1993). Two books by Andrew Gurr are indispensable for an understanding of the prevailing theatrical conditions, *The Shakespearean Stage* 1572–1642 (Cambridge, 1992) and *Play-Going in Shakespeare's London* (Cambridge, 1996).

Most discussions of Shakespeare's moral values assume them to be those of selected characters in his drama and his own religious orientation remains undetermined. Discussions of his ethics are as a consequence few and unconvincing.

As a consequence of the vogue of new historicism, Shakespeare's political thought has received far more attention than his ethics, resulting in a number of impressive volumes such as *Political Shakespeare: Essays in Cultural Materialism* edited by Jonathan Dollimore and

Allan Sinfield (New York, 1994); *Political Shakespeare*, volume 9 of the selection of essays edited by Stephen Orgel published in 1999 in ten volumes with the series title *Shakespeare: The Critical Complex*; *Shakespeare as Political Thinker* edited by John Alvis and Thomas G. West (New York, 2000); and *Shakespeare's Politics* by Allan Bloom and Harry V. Jaffa (Chicago, 1996). Less challenging and possibly more helpful to the lay reader is Robin Headlam Wells, *Shakespeare, Politics, and the State* (Basingstoke, 1986).

Very few commentators deal at length or in depth with Shakespearean teleology. A little known book by T. McAlindon, *Shakespeare's Tragic Cosmos* (Cambridge, 1991), is both accessible and helpful as is the collection of essays in honor of W. R. Elton, edited by John M. Mucciolo, with the title *Shakespeare's Universe: Renaissance Ideas and Conventions* (London, 1996). Readers might find Steven Marx's *Shakespeare and the Bible* (Oxford, 2000) a valuable addition to the standard works on Shakespeare's use of the scriptures.

Shakespeare's notion of society is adumbrated in some of the writing about his politics. Stephen Greenblatt's *Shakespearean Negotiations: The Circulation of Social Energy in Renaissance England* (Berkeley, 1988) is still illuminating. *Shakespeare's Festive World: Elizabethan Seasonal Entertainment and the Professional Stage* (Cambridge, 1991) by Jean-Pierre Laroque promises more than it can deliver, but it does attempt to address the question of the relation of Shakespeare's theater to popular entertainments. A more authoritative treatment of Shakespeare's relationship with popular culture can be found in Annabel Patterson, *Shakespeare and the Popular Voice* (Cambridge, Mass., and Oxford, 1989).

INDEX

•

Page numbers in *italics* include illustrations and photographs/captions.

PICTURE CREDITS

•

BRIEF INSIGHTS

•

A series of concise, engrossing, and enlightening books that explore every subject under the sun with unique insight.

Available now or coming soon: